The

VOLANTE
FARMS

COOKBOOK

Volante Farms
292 Forest Street
Needham, Massachusetts 02492

Printed in the U.S.A.
First Edition
© 2017 Volante Farms Inc.

Book and cover design by Vale Hill Creative www.valehillcreative.com
Design layout by Fyfe Design www.fyfe.com
Photography by Tara Morris www.taramorrisimages.com
Custom publication by Union Park Press www.unionparkpress.com

UNION PARK
PRESS

The VOLANTE FARMS

COOKBOOK

A CENTURY OF GROWING

RYAN CONROY

RECIPES BY TODD
AND JEN HEBERLEIN

NEEDHAM, MASSACHUSETTS

Table of Contents

AN ENDANGERED SPECIES

IN the not too distant past, dozens of family farms dotted the counties surrounding the city of Boston. America was once far more agricultural than it is now. A greater percentage of the population lived off the land when Peter Paul Volante, not yet twenty years old, stepped off the boat that brought him to a new world in 1900. After making a living with hurdy-gurdies and fruit stands, Peter turned to farming. In 1917, what would become Volante Farms came into being. And as one Volante generation gave way to others over the decades, the tradition continued for the next one hundred years.

New England—with its hardscrabble soil and short growing season—does not give generously; it takes hard, labor-intensive work to bring forth its bounty. On a summer's day spent in the fields you can hear the tongues of Asia and Latin America as temporary workers plant and pick the vegetables for your table. Perhaps one or two of them hope to own their own farm one day, as Peter did, for the story of Volante Farms is the immigrant story of America, albeit writ more successfully than most.

In more recent times, the farms of New England have given way to housing tracts and urban sprawl, or have just been abandoned as the tillers moved off the land. The woods of New England are filled with stone walls that farmers—now long forgotten—built and then abandoned along with the land. Creatures like deer and turkeys have returned in great numbers to bedevil farmers as cultivation dwindles.

Yet Volante Farms continues to prosper even as neighboring farms have vanished. Today, customers at the farm can find everything from prepared meals and wine to fresh farm products and Christmas trees. There can be no doubt that vegetables grown in the neighborhood are far tastier than those of vast agri-businesses that have to travel thousands of miles to reach your table. It would be a pity indeed were family farms to vanish forever from the Eastern Seaboard.

In the beginning of our nation's story, most New Englanders were either farmers or fishermen, but now both industries are greatly diminished. Family farms should be considered a national asset as well as an endangered species to be protected and preserved for the common good.

-HDS Greenway

DEDICATION

WHEN we first set out to celebrate our farm's centennial we wanted to find a way to share with you the history of our family and our business, two stories that are as intertwined as the crops we grow and the food we create. As a result, this book is at once our family's journey, a field guide to our produce, and a wealth of recipes that are meant to be shared and savored among family and friends.

Unless otherwise noted, the recipes that follow are from Chef Todd Heberlein and Pastry Chef Jen Heberlein, who developed these beautiful dishes while sharing space in the farm's rapidly expanding kitchen.

This book is dedicated to the community that comprises Volante Farms, from the generations before us, to the loyal staff that has kept us going, to the customers who have supported us throughout the decades, and to our fellow local farmers who continue their tireless work year in and year out. Salud!

-Dave, Teri & Steve

VOLANTE FARMS

— Spring —

PETER & CATERINA

Peter P. Volante holding his famous
Pascal Celery, 1930s.

Peter and Caterina, 1930s.

ATINA, ITALY 1881

High in the western foothills of the central Apennines—halfway between Rome to the north and Naples to the south—sits the ancient city of Atina. With a history that predates Rome, the fortified octagonal stone walls have witnessed the comings and goings of countless generations and all manners of economic and political waves.

The Volante Farms story begins here, at the home of Alphonse and Maria, with the birth of Peter Paul Volante in 1881. Peter quickly grew into an affable young man, known for his smile. Life in the small bucolic village held limited opportunities, so after a short stint with the Italian Bicycle Infantry, he set out for America in 1900.

He found work in Newton, Massachusetts helping to construct the new Mason School in Newton Centre, a school his children would later attend. After saving three hundred dollars, he returned to Italy to marry Caterina Lanni. By 1903 they had begun to work their way back to Massachusetts, making a stop in Scotland on the way, where Caterina's family was in the ice cream business.

Peter and Caterina settled in Brighton, Massachusetts and were immersed in the typical immigrant experience: struggling for acceptance, finding comfort in the companionship of their countrymen, and seeking all available opportunities. Peter had a run at organ grinding, a specialty of the Italians from his province, before ultimately finding work at various neighborhood fruit stands.

Eventually Peter secured employment at the Stone Family Farm in the Newton village of Oak Hill in 1915. The fifty-acre farm sat atop a knoll that now overlooks the Charles River Country Club. The Stones, whose family had held the land since colonial times, did not have heirs interested in continuing the agricultural tradition, which provided Peter with a unique opportunity.

Peter learned the farming business quickly and secured a mortgage from an Italian-friendly bank in

Newton's Nonantum neighborhood. He purchased the farm and the accompanying farmhouse at 391 Dedham Street from the Stones in 1917. From there, Peter started the business that was the Volantes' first foray into farming on American soil: P. Volante Market Gardener.

As a market farmer, Peter delivered his crops—mostly broccoli, tomatoes, and celery—to markets in Boston. He purchased a new REO Speedwagon with roll-up canvas sides and loaded it daily with produce. Caterina would either ride into town with him or stay behind, perched on a wooden box under an umbrella to keep a watchful and stern eye over the field crew.

As the business and the family grew, Peter sought more farmland. He joined forces with a relative on a farm in Rhode Island for a time. He also embarked on an odd annual pilgrimage with a contingent of Yankee farmers. As the frost began to fall on Massachusetts farms, the Volantes' tractors and other equipment would be loaded onto the Seaboard Air Line Railroad's freight train cars. The tropically hued diesel engines of trains like the Orange Blossom Special would transport Peter's equipment and crew to and from Florida seasonally. This also meant the Volantes could make the pilgrimage for at least part of the season and sneak in a little vacation for the kids. By March, the annual harvest in the South would be well underway, and by the end of the month, the equipment would be headed north again to break ground in Newton. As cross-country transportation became cheaper, the advent of large-scale California agriculture made this method of double-cropping untenable.

Clockwise from top left: Peter's REO Speedwagon, 1920s; the produce market, 1920s; Peter and crew planting celery in Florida, 1940s.

PASCAL

CELERY

Peter P. Volante's
Special Strain
SUMMER PASCAL
CELERY SEED

THE ORIGINAL PURE STRAIN MEANS BIG-GER CROPS OF HIGHER QUALITY

PRICE, $15.00 per lb.
50 lbs. or more $12.50 per lb.

Peter P. Volante
391 Dedham Street
NEWTON CENTER 59, MASS.

Clockwise from top left: Celery label, 1930s; Margie's original farmstand, 1950s; Peter Volante's Pascal Celery Seed ad, 1947; Ferdinand Volante with tomato boxes still used today, 1960; Peter in the celery field, 1940s; Peter the celery king, 1930s; Margie and the hotbeds, 1950s. Center: Peter growing Comet Tomatoes, 1950s.

The family's success with the farm allowed them the opportunity to raise and educate seven children—four daughters and three sons. In a time when women's education wasn't deemed necessary, Peter found it important to send his daughters to esteemed colleges. Rose and Anne attended Wellesley College, and Margie and Helen went to Regis College. Helen joined the Sisters of St. Joseph after graduation. The men of the family were also well educated, with William and Mario attending the Massachusetts Institute of Technology and Alfred studying at Boston College.

On a trip south in 1941, Peter found himself in the good graces of a Pennsylvania Dutch farmer. Peter managed—through kindness or payment, it is unclear which—to part this particular farmer with a tightly held secret of the region: the source of Pascal Celery. Pennsylvania Dutch farmers in the Lancaster area had dominated the East Coast celery market since the turn of the century, and the seed source was closely guarded "in a manner reminiscent of the vigilantes of old" (Everett Smith; *Christian Science Monitor*, September 2, 1953). Peter's procurement of these celery seeds marked a turning point for Volante Farms. He developed it into the most successful celery seed in the region for years to come. Peter Volante's trademarked Summer Pascal Celery seed remained preeminent in the eastern United States until a larger variety from Utah replaced it in the mid-1950s.

After World War II, Americans embraced a slew of opportunities and lifestyle changes. The wave of prosperity that followed the war caused Americans to change the way they shopped and how they ate. Access to cars and the ensuing migration to the suburbs led to large grocery stores, packaged foods, and a penchant for convenience.

Peter's daughter, Margie, noticed these new trends and saw an opportunity for growth. In 1949, she opened the first roadside stand at the Newton farm, which was essentially a collection of wooden boxes and tables. There was no roof or tent to provide cover; workers just pulled a tarp over the tables in inclement weather. The stand was set in the front lawn of the Dedham Street house. Within ten years, the popularity of the farmstand would make Peter's daily trips to the Boston market obsolete, and the stand would grow into a substantial building with legitimate walls, roof, and a wooden floor.

Peter passed away in 1953 with Caterina following him in 1967. He is still remembered as a charismatic man who expected hard work, supported his family at all costs, and always enjoyed a cigar. During his lifetime he built the backbone for an ever-changing business in a community that was looking at food in a whole new way.

A 1940s family photo, left to right: Mario, Rose, William, Alfred, Caterina, Helen, Peter, Anne, and cousin Bessie.

SPRING

BEFORE THE LAST snowbanks melt away and the frozen fields become a muddy expanse, the first colors of spring emerge in the greenhouse. Vibrant pots of pansies line the aisles alongside vegetable seedlings, which are patiently waiting to be transplanted. Once the ground has thawed completely, we plow and harrow space for our first field crops of the year. Our goal is to get the peas in the ground around St. Patrick's Day, with corn following shortly thereafter. The field crew protects these crops by laying down floating row covers, which are huge paper-like sheets that keep plants warm and sheltered in the cool New England spring. The first crates of asparagus, lettuce, radishes, and spinach start to filter into the farmstand in April, marking the beginning of another season's harvest.

Spring Pea and Asparagus Soup, page 21.

Spring Recipes

SPRING PEA *and* **ASPARAGUS SOUP**
SPINACH SALAD *with* **STRAWBERRIES** *and* **STRAWBERRY VINAIGRETTE**
ASPARAGUS SALAD *with* **BEET RELISH**

·

PARSNIP *and* **BLARNEY CHEESE TART**
POTATO *and* **DANDELION GREEN GRATIN**
SWEET PEA *and* **GARLIC SCAPE PESTO**

·

GRILLED COD *with* **GRILLED RADISH SALSA**
SPRING DUG PARSNIP GNOCCHI *with* **SPRING VEGETABLES**

·

RHUBARB *and* **THYME JAM**
HONEY PINE NUT TARTS *with* **STRAWBERRIES** *and* **RHUBARB**
WHITE CHOCOLATE RHUBARB SCONES
SHORTCAKES *with* **WHIPPED CREAM**
CARROT WHOOPIE PIES
CREAM CHEESE FROSTING

·

SOUTHSIDE

Produce Spotlight
ASPARAGUS

ASPARAGUS is a recent addition to the farm's produce lineup. Prior to constructing the year-round farmstand, we sought ways to extend the harvest season and provide home-grown produce for a longer stretch of time. While we previously spent our springs focusing on greenhouse operations, now we could consider a spring harvest season as well.

We had recently acquired access to more land at the Greenway fields and were looking to revert more of it back into cultivation. We prepped about three acres with rich compost and cut deep trenches for the asparagus crowns.

Asparagus crops take several years to mature and can't be picked heavily for the first three seasons. Once established, however, crops can last for upwards of twenty years. As with any new crop, we consulted with other local farmers regarding their experiences. Sage advice from Steve Verrill of Verrill Farm was invaluable in getting this crop off to a good start.

Asparagus is now the first of our homegrown produce to reach the stand in the spring. Each stalk has to be cut shortly after the first thick spears thrust through the cool soil, as they grow several inches per day. If we are too slow to harvest, the tips will unfurl their fern-like leaves and render them unmarketable. We snap or slice them off just below the surface, quickly turning a recently harvested row into a seemingly empty field.

Our harvest begins in late April and lasts well into June. After the harvest peaks, we let the last spears fulfill their desire to leaf out. The four-foot-tall fronds create fields of beautiful green ferns that take over the space through the summer. As they turn brown come fall, they are mowed down, and we wait for next spring.

SPRING PEA *and* ASPARAGUS SOUP

When fresh, asparagus is tender and sweet enough to eat raw and requires almost no trimming prior to cooking. If you can't get freshly picked asparagus, make sure to trim off any of the fibrous, woody bits that can develop when cut stalks sit for too long. An easy trick is just to snap each stalk in your hands; they tend to break right above where the dry part ends, though a knife works as well.

SERVES 4 TO 6

1 bunch scallions

1 pound English peas, shelled, pods reserved

2 quarts chicken stock

2 cups water

Kosher salt, to taste

Black pepper, to taste

2 tablespoons salted butter

2 pounds asparagus, trimmed, cut into 1-inch pieces

1 cup crème fraîche

1 tablespoon chopped tarragon

1 teaspoon lemon zest

Chop the scallions, setting aside the white parts.

Make stock. Add pea pods, scallion greens, chicken stock, water, and a pinch of salt and pepper to a large pot and bring to a boil. Immediately reduce heat and simmer for 20 minutes.

While stock simmers, melt butter in a large pot over medium heat. Add scallion whites and cook for 6 to 8 minutes.

After 20 minutes, remove stock from heat, strain, discard solids, and set aside liquid. Add stock to cooked scallions and bring to a boil. Reduce heat to a simmer and add asparagus, peas, and a pinch of salt and pepper. Simmer until vegetables are tender, about 10 to 12 minutes. Remove from heat.

Purée soup in the pot with an immersion blender. If you don't have an immersion blender, purée in small batches in a traditional blender and return the soup to the pot. (Be careful; the soup is hot!) Season to taste with salt and pepper.

Mix together the crème fraîche, tarragon, and lemon zest. Pour soup into bowls and add a dollop of crème fraîche mixture to each bowl.

CHEF'S NOTE: *Reserve a handful of cooked peas or asparagus pieces to use as a garnish. Their vibrant color really brings the season to the table.*

SPINACH SALAD *with* STRAWBERRIES *and* STRAWBERRY VINAIGRETTE

We are big fans of simple salads—and this one is as simple as it is refreshing. Strawberries are sweetest during late spring, so we want to take full advantage of their flavor. This vinaigrette is the perfect way to showcase these delightful red berries in a savory dish.

SERVES 4 TO 6

STRAWBERRY VINAIGRETTE

2 tablespoons
balsamic vinegar

1 teaspoon Dijon mustard

1 tablespoon honey

Kosher salt, to taste

Black pepper, to taste

1 pint strawberries (about
2 cups), tops removed

½ cup extra virgin olive oil

SPINACH SALAD

¾ cup sliced almonds

8 ounces baby spinach

1 quart strawberries (about
4 cups), tops removed,
quartered

5 ounces goat cheese,
crumbled

Preheat oven to 350°F.

Place almonds on a sheet pan and toast until golden brown, about 8 to 10 minutes.

Make vinaigrette. Add vinegar, mustard, honey, and a pinch of salt and pepper to a blender and pulse for 20 seconds. Add strawberries and pulse for another 30 seconds.

Keep blender running and slowly add olive oil until combined. Adjust seasoning to taste with salt and pepper and set aside completed vinaigrette. This vinaigrette will keep in the refrigerator for up to 1 week.

Prepare salad. Divide spinach onto plates and top with cut strawberries, almonds, and goat cheese.

Drizzle with vinaigrette and enjoy as a refreshing first course or as a meal by itself.

SPINACH

Spinach is traditionally best suited to cooler growing temperatures, but we seek out varieties that will stretch through spring, summer, and into the fall. The first spinach to arrive in spring is the crop seeded the previous October. The dormant plants green up quickly under the first warm rays of spring sun, while freshly seeded green and red spinach cautiously poke out tender leaves in the weeks following.

ASPARAGUS SALAD *with* BEET RELISH

This salad has everything you need for a fabulous spring dinner: bitter greens, sweet asparagus, salty cheese, tart beets, and bright citrus flavor. The sourdough croutons add texture and depth to this dish, making it hearty and filling.

SERVES 4 TO 6

1 pound asparagus

Kosher salt, to taste

Black pepper, to taste

3 tablespoons olive oil

4 ounces arugula

2 ounces dandelion greens

2 cups torn sourdough bread (crouton-sized pieces)

Zest of 1 orange

4 ounces goat's milk feta, crumbled

2 tablespoons Beet Relish, plus liquid for drizzling

Place a sheet pan in the oven and preheat to 425°F.

Trim asparagus, place in a large bowl, and season with salt and pepper. Drizzle with olive oil and mix together, thoroughly coating asparagus.

Remove preheated pan from oven and carefully spread asparagus in one layer on the hot pan. Return pan to oven and cook for about 8 to 10 minutes. Remove from oven and set aside.

Mix together arugula and dandelion greens and arrange on a large platter. Scatter asparagus and torn bread over the greens. Sprinkle with orange zest and feta.

Spoon Beet Relish on top of the salad, drizzle a tablespoon of the liquid from the Beet Relish over the greens, and serve family style.

BEET RELISH

This is essentially a beet-infused vinaigrette with a dual purpose. You get both a delicious, unique dressing and a crunchy, bright garnish in one recipe. Trust us on keeping the beets raw; they're incredible.

MAKES ABOUT 2 CUPS

1 medium red, Chiogga, or golden beet, rinsed and greens discarded

1½ teaspoons Dijon mustard

2 tablespoons sherry vinegar

⅓ cup extra virgin olive oil

3 scallions, white parts only, diced

2 tablespoons chopped parsley

Kosher salt, to taste

Black pepper, to taste

Peel beet and dice into pieces about the size of corn kernels (they will be raw, so size is important) and set aside.

In a bowl, whisk together mustard and vinegar. Continue whisking and slowly add olive oil. Fold in scallions, parsley, and beets and season to taste with salt and pepper. Transfer to a glass or plastic sealable container.

Refrigerate for 1 to 2 hours to allow flavors to develop before using.

This relish will keep in the refrigerator for up to 1 week.

PARSNIP *and* BLARNEY CHEESE TART

SERVES 4 TO 6

CRUST

2 sticks salted butter, cubed, at room temperature

8 ounces cream cheese

2 cups all-purpose flour, plus more for rolling out

¼ teaspoon kosher salt

Pinch of black pepper

FILLING

2 parsnips (about ½ pound), peeled

4 tablespoons olive oil, divided

Kosher salt, to taste

Black pepper, to taste

2 medium yellow onions (about 1 pound), thinly sliced

8 ounces kale, chopped

1 egg

½ cup buttermilk

7 ounces blarney cheese, shredded (or substitute gouda or gruyère)

Make crust. Place butter in the bowl of an electric stand mixer fitted with paddle attachment. Mix at medium speed for 1 minute. Add cream cheese and mix for an additional minute. Slowly add in dry ingredients and mix until dough forms, about 5 to 6 minutes, scraping down the sides of the bowl periodically.

Place dough on a lightly floured surface and form into a 1-inch-thick disk. Wrap in plastic and refrigerate for 15 minutes.

Remove dough from refrigerator and place on a floured surface. Using a rolling pin, roll dough out to ¼-inch thickness, adding small amounts of flour to prevent sticking. The finished circle should be about 11 inches in diameter.

Place dough in a 9-inch tart pan and press down into the shape of the pan, trimming off any excess. Freeze the dough-lined pan for 1 hour.

Preheat oven to 400°F. Remove dough from freezer, press foil tightly onto dough, being sure to completely cover edges. Fill with pie weights or dried beans to prevent bubbling up while cooking.

Bake for 15 minutes. Remove from oven, lift off foil, and gently press down with a paper towel anywhere the dough has risen.

Return crust to oven and continue to bake until golden brown, another 8 to 10 minutes. Remove from oven and let cool.

Lower the oven temperature to 350°F.

Prepare parsnips. Slice them lengthwise, and then slice thinly into half-moons. Toss with 2 tablespoons olive oil and a pinch of salt and pepper. Lay the parsnips flat on a sheet pan, roast until just tender, about 15 minutes, and set aside.

Make filling. Heat the remaining olive oil in a large sauté pan over medium-high heat. Add onions and cook until golden brown, about 10 to 12 minutes. Add kale and cook until wilted, another 6 to 8 minutes. Season to taste with salt and pepper and let cool for 10 minutes.

In a bowl, beat egg and add buttermilk. Incorporate the onion and kale mixture, add cheese, and season to taste with salt and pepper.

Arrange parsnips on the bottom of the crust. Pour in the filling and spread evenly.

Bake until tart has set and is golden brown, about 25 minutes.

Let cool and enjoy for breakfast, brunch, or as a decadent side dish at dinner!

POTATO *and* DANDELION GREEN GRATIN

The Catalogna dandelions we grow on the farm are not the same horrid weeds that dot your lawn each spring. Our flowers are in the chicory family and look more like cornflowers, with deep blue blossoms perched on top of gangly stalks in late summer. The leaves are a highly prized green with a bitter taste—like many of the best Italian greens—and are quick to grow in the springtime. They are the perfect sharp addition to a sandwich or salad in need of a spark of flavor. Ferdinand was a huge fan of the dandelions and would anticipate their arrival in early spring.

SERVES 6 TO 8

1 red bell pepper, halved and deseeded

1 teaspoon plus 2 tablespoons olive oil, divided

1 teaspoon kosher salt, plus more to taste

Black pepper, to taste

2 tablespoons salted butter

1 medium yellow onion, thinly sliced

1 tablespoon chopped garlic

1 cup grape tomatoes (about ½ pint), halved

8 ounces dandelion greens

2 pounds Yukon gold potatoes, peeled

2 cups light cream

1 cup plain breadcrumbs

3½ tablespoons olive tapenade (store bought)

Preheat oven to 400°F.

Toss bell pepper with 1 teaspoon olive oil and a pinch of salt and pepper. Roast on a sheet pan for 18 to 20 minutes until skin starts to blister. Remove from oven and let cool. Remove skin, dice pepper into 1-inch chunks, and set aside.

Melt butter in a large sauté pan over medium-high heat. Add onions and cook until golden brown, about 12 to 15 minutes. Add garlic and cook for 1 minute, stirring. Add tomatoes and cook for 10 minutes. Remove pan from heat.

Remove and discard the bottom inch of the dandelion green stems. Roughly chop the remaining greens and place in a large bowl.

Thinly slice potatoes either by hand or with a mandoline, keeping the thickness uniform. Add to dandelion greens along with roasted peppers and onion mixture. Mix together with 1 teaspoon salt and pinch of pepper.

Lower oven temperature to 350°F.

Grease a 9-by-13-inch baking dish with butter or cooking spray and add the potato mixture and enough cream to just cover the mixture. Cover dish with foil and cook until potatoes are tender, about 35 to 40 minutes.

While the potato mixture cooks, mix together the breadcrumbs, tapenade, and remaining olive oil.

When potatoes are tender, remove baking dish from oven and discard foil. Evenly sprinkle the breadcrumb mixture on top of the bubbling potatoes. Return dish to oven and bake uncovered until the breadcrumbs are golden brown, about 10 to 12 minutes.

Remove from oven and serve warm.

PEAS

SPRING peas—or English peas—are the quintessential spring vegetable. Sometime in early March, the field crew starts to prepare for the first pea crop, which we hope to have planted by St. Patrick's Day. We have a long-standing (and friendly) rivalry with Marini Farm in Ipswich over who plants and picks their peas first. Whether planting or picking is more important depends on if we are winning, of course.

Like all of our crops, the peas are handpicked with care, allowing us to closely monitor the quality. On late-spring days, all available hands head out to the field with bushel baskets in tow to pore over the rows and pop off the full pods.

RADISHES

RADISHES are perfect for farmers who love immediate gratification. We directly seed them in the field every ten days or so from April through October and harvest them about a month after planting. Their speed and reliable germination make them a satisfying crop to grow.

These spicy spheres of red, white, and purple offer a bite that is a far cry from watery, tasteless salad bar radishes. Fresh from the fields, our radishes are perfect sliced on top of a salad or as a simple antipasto dressed with oil, a dash of light vinegar, and salt. The beautiful, cylindrical French breakfast radishes are great when served on toast with a dab of good butter or braised in springtime pastas. For the best breakfast radish experience, however, pop one from the soil early in the morning, brush off the dirt on a shirttail, and take a zesty bite.

SWEET PEA *and* GARLIC SCAPE PESTO

In the springtime, peas are so sweet they can be devoured straight from the field. Handing guests a bowl of uncooked peas, however, doesn't always go over well. Don't worry. There is a way to give them that fresh-from-the-garden taste with a minimal amount of cooking.

Anytime we cook peas at the farm, we preserve their flavor and color by blanching them. It's pretty simple. After boiling your peas for a short time, strain them and then immediately plunge them into an ice bath, which will instantly stop the cooking process. Voila! That fresh color and taste stays intact.

MAKES ABOUT 2 CUPS

2 pounds English peas

3 tablespoons pine nuts

Kosher salt, to taste

¼ cup chopped garlic scapes

½ cup grated
Parmesan cheese

1 cup basil leaves

½ cup extra virgin olive oil

Black pepper, to taste

Preheat oven to 350°F.

Shell the peas and discard the pods.

Place pine nuts on a dry sheet pan and toast in oven for 8 to 10 minutes until golden.

Fill a large bowl with ice water and set aside.

Bring a pot of salted water to a boil. Drop peas into water and cook until just tender, about 2½ to 3 minutes.

Strain peas and immediately submerge into the bowl of ice water.

Put garlic scapes, pine nuts, and cheese into a food processor. Pulse until a paste is formed. Add peas, basil, olive oil, and a pinch of salt and pepper. Pulse until smooth.

This versatile pesto is great in pasta, on pizza, over eggs, and spread over pita with grilled vegetables.

GRILLED COD *with* GRILLED RADISH SALSA

Radishes are one of the few vegetables that seem to grow well for us in any type of weather. Successfully growing and stockpiling radishes means we continuously come up with unique ways to prepare this gem of a vegetable. Grilling them is one of our favorite methods.

In this dish, the fat in the cod complements this salsa incredibly well, but if you are making the salsa without the fish, add a diced avocado before serving. The creaminess of the avocado will give the salsa a smooth finish.

SERVES 4

2 pounds radishes (any variety), tops discarded

7 tablespoons olive oil, divided

Kosher salt, to taste

Black pepper, to taste

1 cup diced cucumber, deseeded (burpless works well here)

2 cups chopped scallions

1 tablespoon chopped cilantro

2 tablespoons lime juice

1 tablespoon jalapenos, deseeded and diced

2 pounds cod, cut into 4 pieces

Preheat grill to medium-high.

In a bowl, lightly coat radishes with 3 tablespoons olive oil and a pinch of salt and pepper. Grill the radishes as evenly as possible until the skins are nicely charred. Remove from heat and let cool.

Cut radishes into a small dice and add to a bowl along with cucumbers, scallions, cilantro, lime juice, jalapeños, and a pinch of salt and pepper. Set aside.

Place each piece of cod in the center of a large square of foil. Season each piece with 1 tablespoon olive oil and a pinch of salt and pepper. Fold foil over fish, making a packet with the seam on the side (not the top or bottom). Grill fish for 10 to 15 minutes, flipping halfway through, until thoroughly cooked (grill time may vary depending on the thickness of filets).

Remove fish from grill, unwrap foil, and plate with radish salsa spooned over top. Enjoy!

SPRING DUG PARSNIP GNOCCHI *with* SPRING VEGETABLES

Parsnips are the unsung heroes of the farm kitchen. We get them homegrown twice a year: first in the fall, when they find their way into countless holiday dishes, and later in the spring, when the cold has tempered their starches into delightfully sweet sugar. These gnocchi are best with those sweet, spring parsnips. It's a great twist on a classic dish that will have you rethinking the parsnip entirely.

SERVES 4 TO 6

GNOCCHI

4 tablespoons olive oil, divided

4 parsnips (about 1 pound), peeled and chopped into 2-inch pieces

Kosher salt, to taste

Black pepper, to taste

2 eggs

2 cups all-purpose flour

2 tablespoons chopped chives

⅓ cup grated Romano cheese

SPRING VEGETABLES

2 tablespoons olive oil, divided

1 leek, white part only, diced

1 tablespoon chopped garlic

½ cup white wine

1½ cups reserved cooking liquid from gnocchi

1 pound asparagus, trimmed and thinly sliced

4 ounces baby spinach

½ cup grated Romano cheese

1 tablespoon chopped parsley

1 teaspoon lemon zest

Kosher salt, to taste

Black pepper, to taste

Heat 2 tablespoons olive oil in a large pot over medium-high heat. Add parsnips and cook until lightly browned on all sides, about 10 to 12 minutes.

Add a pinch of salt and pepper and enough water to just cover the parsnips. Bring to a boil and then immediately reduce to a simmer. Cook until parsnips are a bit beyond fork tender (they need to be soft enough to mash), about 20 minutes. Drain and reserve liquid. Let parsnips cool completely.

Place parsnips into a food processor and purée. Add eggs and pulse for 20 seconds.

Transfer to a bowl and add flour, chives, cheese, and pinch of salt and pepper. Knead dough and form into a ball. Wrap in plastic and refrigerate for 1 to 2 hours.

Lightly flour a work surface. Divide dough into 3 pieces. Roll each piece into a 1-inch-thick rope. Cut ropes into 1-inch pieces and set aside.

Bring reserved parsnip liquid to a boil in a large pot with a pinch of salt, adding water so that the pot is ⅔ full.

Working in 2 batches, drop gnocchi into liquid and cook. When gnocchi floats to the surface, remove with a slotted spoon or strainer and let drain. Spread cooked gnocchi over a sheet pan drizzled with remaining olive oil to prevent sticking. When both batches are done, reserve 1½ cups cooking liquid.

Prepare vegetables. Heat 1 tablespoon olive oil in a large pan over medium heat. Add leeks and cook until soft, about 6 to 8 minutes. Add garlic and cook for 2 minutes.

Add wine and reduce by half, about 4 to 5 minutes. Add reserved cooking liquid and simmer for 5 minutes.

Add asparagus and gnocchi and simmer for 1 minute. Remove from heat.

Fold in spinach, cheese, remaining oil, parsley, and lemon zest. Season to taste with salt and pepper.

RHUBARB

THE leaves of this perennial vegetable peek out of the soil shortly after the daffodils start to bloom. As the plants grow to a height of a few feet with leaves the size of platters, the stalks begin to turn red. The crowns send up beautiful spikes with fragile white flower clusters, which are unceremoniously chopped off and discarded to help the plant concentrate its energy into edible stalk formation. The stalks come off the crown with a satisfactory pop when they are ready to harvest. The inedible leaves are sliced off in the field, leaving the stalks with just a touch of green to show the freshness of the pick.

RHUBARB *and* THYME JAM

Though rhubarb is frequently cooked down with strawberries, there is more to this oddball, early spring vegetable. This recipe brings out the best in the funky reddish stalks and transforms them into a delightful, savory spread with endless applications. Try it with biscuits, English muffins, baked brie, or on roasted pork.

MAKES ABOUT 2½ CUPS

¼ cup white wine

2 sprigs thyme

½ tablespoon minced crystallized ginger

1 piece star anise

Pinch of black pepper

½ cup orange juice

2 cups (about ½ pound) rhubarb, thinly sliced

1 tablespoon Ball classic pectin

2½ cups granulated sugar

Add white wine, thyme, ginger, star anise, and pepper to a saucepot over medium heat. Reduce until only a few tablespoons of liquid remain, 8 to 10 minutes. Add orange juice and reduce by half, about 3 to 5 minutes. Add rhubarb and pectin and bring to a boil.

Slowly whisk in sugar. Bring to a boil again for 1 minute, careful not to let it boil over, and then remove from heat. Skim off any foam and discard the star anise and thyme. Pour hot mixture into canning jars and leave uncovered until cool.

This jam will keep in a sealed jar for up to 3 months.

CHEF'S NOTE: *There are numerous brands and varieties of pectin available at grocery stores and online. Different brands may require different ratios of pectin per batch and may yield varying results. If possible, use Ball classic pectin for this recipe. Otherwise, just make sure the pectin is not a "no sugar" or "instant" variety, as these require very different applications.*

HONEY PINE NUT TARTS *with* STRAWBERRIES *and* RHUBARB

MAKES 12 TO 16 TARTS

CRUST

1½ cups all-purpose flour

⅓ cup granulated sugar

¼ teaspoon iodized salt

1¼ teaspoons baking powder

8 tablespoons salted butter, cubed, cold

2 tablespoons lemon zest

1 teaspoon vanilla extract

2 tablespoons water

1 egg

FILLING

1½ cups pine nuts

2 cups (about 1 pound) chopped rhubarb

½ pint (about 1 cup) sliced strawberries

½ cup granulated sugar, divided

2 tablespoons lemon juice

½ cup heavy cream

2 eggs

⅔ cup honey

1 teaspoon kosher salt

1½ sticks salted butter

Make crust. Place flour, sugar, salt, baking powder, butter, and lemon zest in a food processor. Pulse until the mixture resembles small peas.

Transfer to a bowl, add vanilla extract, water, and egg, and knead into a ball. Refrigerate dough for at least 1 hour (the dough can be made a day ahead).

Preheat oven to 325°F.

Place pine nuts on a dry sheet pan and toast for 8 to 10 minutes until golden.

Make filling. Add rhubarb, strawberries, ¼ cup sugar, and lemon juice to a saucepan. Simmer on low until mushy and liquid is slightly reduced, about 15 to 20 minutes. Set aside and let cool completely.

Whisk together cream and eggs and set aside.

Add honey, remaining sugar, salt, and butter to a saucepan and bring to a boil, stirring constantly. Boil gently for 2 minutes, then remove from heat and let cool for about 15 minutes. Whisk together cream mixture and warm honey mixture.

Grease a muffin pan with butter or cooking spray. Remove dough from refrigerator and roll it out until it is ¼-inch thick. Cut out circles that are about 1 inch larger than the circumference of the muffin cavity and press each gently into prepared muffin pan. Freeze for at least 10 minutes or until ready to use, otherwise the tart shells will shrink when baked. When ready to bake, place the muffin pan on a sheet pan so that any filling that bubbles over doesn't make a mess.

Spoon 1 tablespoon of rhubarb mixture into the bottom of each tart shell. Distribute pine nuts equally among the tart shells. Finish by filling each tart shell to the top with the honey mixture. Bake tarts until golden and bubbly, about 35 to 45 minutes.

Remove from oven and let cool completely before unmolding.

Serve at room temperature.

WHITE CHOCOLATE RHUBARB SCONES

MAKES 8 SCONES

2⅓ cups all-purpose flour, plus more for rolling out

3 tablespoons granulated sugar, plus more for sprinkling

1 tablespoon baking powder

1 teaspoon iodized salt

6 tablespoons salted butter, cubed, cold

2 teaspoons lemon zest, finely grated

½ cup white chocolate, chopped into ¼-inch pieces

1 cup (about ¼ pound) rhubarb, chopped into ¼-inch pieces

½ cup whole milk, cold

½ cup heavy cream, plus more for brushing

2 teaspoons vanilla extract

Preheat oven to 375°F and line a baking sheet with parchment paper.

Put flour, sugar, baking powder, and salt in a food processor. Pulse once or twice to combine. Add butter and lemon zest and pulse until butter is incorporated and mixture resembles a coarse meal.

Dump mixture into a large mixing bowl. Stir in chocolate and rhubarb.

Working quickly and gently, stir in milk, cream, and vanilla extract. Be careful not to overwork the dough!

Form dough into a flat disc approximately 1-inch thick, sprinkling with additional flour if it is too sticky to handle. Cut into 8 equal wedges.

Brush each wedge with cream, sprinkle with granulated sugar, and place on lined baking sheet. Bake for 12 minutes, rotate the pan, and continue baking for about 10 more minutes. Scones are done when they are golden brown and spring back when pressed gently in the middle.

CHEF'S NOTE: *For a real treat, mix equal parts Rhubarb and Thyme Jam (pg. 40) and mascarpone and spread liberally onto the scones.*

STRAWBERRIES

STRAWBERRIES are one of the few fruits that garner space in our vegetable fields. We can harvest a strawberry crop for two to three years, picking a few overlapping crops in the same season.

As soon as we escape the threat of overnight frosts in early spring, we plant the bare roots in wide rows with leafless crowns just peeking above the soil. With a few warm days and a little rain, the leaves begin to flush out. A week or so later, tiny yellow flowers with creamy white petals appear. We walk through the rows, plucking these away, coaxing the plants to put their energy toward establishing roots. We do not count on a strong harvest in the first year.

Throughout the summer, we cultivate for weeds and irrigate the plants while harvesting the previous years' crops. The crew heads out to the field with quart boxes, handpicking the berries. Strawberry picking is slow, and sorting the ripe from the unripe takes a keen eye and practiced hand.

The sun-ripened fruit is often still warm when it reaches the stand, the sweet fragrance sitting in the air like soft perfume in the first weeks of June. Though the season is short, a local berry at its summer peak is unbeatable. After the season wanes, we continue to weed the crop until the fall. Then, sometime in November or December, usually while a trailer of Christmas trees is unloaded in the distance, the field crew covers the plants with a load of saltmarsh hay to keep the berries from freezing and thawing over the long winter and to protect the leaves from hungry deer.

SHORTCAKES *with* WHIPPED CREAM

MAKES 14 TO 16 SHORTCAKES

SHORTCAKES

4½ cups all-purpose flour

2 tablespoons baking powder

1 teaspoon iodized salt

⅔ cup granulated sugar

4 tablespoons salted butter, cold

4 tablespoons vegetable shortening

1 cup heavy cream

1 cup whole milk

1 tablespoon vanilla extract

Coarse or fine sugar, to taste

WHIPPED CREAM

1 cup heavy cream

2 tablespoons granulated sugar

1 teaspoon vanilla extract

Preheat oven to 350°F.

Make the shortcakes. In a large bowl, whisk together flour, baking powder, salt, and sugar. Using a pastry blender or fork, cut butter and shortening into the dry ingredients and mix until incorporated and the mixture resembles small peas.

Add cream, milk, and vanilla extract to the bowl and stir until just combined. Do not overwork the dough or the shortcakes will be tough. The batter should be thick and moist all the way through. If it is too dry, add a little more cream or milk.

Scoop batter with an ice cream scoop (a ⅓-cup measuring cup will work, too) onto a parchment-lined baking sheet. Leave about an inch between the shortcakes. Brush the tops with heavy cream and sprinkle liberally with sugar.

Bake shortcakes for 15 minutes, rotate pan, and continue baking until golden brown on top and cooked through, about 10 additional minutes. Remove from oven and cool to room temperature.

Make whipped cream. Pour cream into a mixing bowl. Using a hand mixer or stand mixer with whip attachment, whip cream until it starts to thicken, about 1 to 2 minutes. Add sugar and vanilla extract and continue whipping until stiff peaks form. Be careful not to over whip or mixture will separate and get lumpy.

Cut the shortcakes in half and serve topped with whipped cream and seasonal fruit.

CARROT WHOOPIE PIES

½ cup hazelnuts

3 cups all-purpose flour

1½ teaspoons baking powder

1 teaspoon baking soda

1 tablespoon ground cinnamon

1 teaspoon ground nutmeg

Pinch of ground cloves

½ teaspoon iodized salt

½ cup granulated sugar

1 cup light brown sugar

4 eggs

1½ cups vegetable oil

2½ cups (about 1 pound) carrots, peeled and grated

1 recipe Cream Cheese Frosting

½ cup cinnamon sugar (See Chef's Note)

Preheat oven to 325°F.

Place hazelnuts on baking sheet, roast for 8 to 10 minutes, remove from oven, chop, and set aside.

In a bowl, stir together flour, baking powder, baking soda, cinnamon, nutmeg, cloves, and salt and set aside.

In a separate bowl, mix together granulated sugar, brown sugar, and eggs. Using a hand mixer or stand mixer fitted with the paddle attachment, whip on medium speed until fully combined, about 2 minutes. Turn mixer to high speed and slowly drizzle in oil. Once oil is incorporated, continue to mix on high until the mixture is light and fluffy, another 2 minutes.

Reduce speed to low and mix in grated carrots. Add dry ingredients and mix until just combined, about 2 minutes. Scrape bowl well to ensure there are no pockets of dry ingredients at the bottom of the bowl.

Line a baking sheet with parchment paper. Drop batter by the tablespoonful onto the baking sheet, leaving about an inch in between each dollop. They will not be perfectly round, but try to keep a uniform size so that they will match up when assembling the pies.

Drop a dollop of Cream Cheese Frosting (about 1 tablespoon) onto the flat side of half of the whoopie pies. Sprinkle frosting with a few hazelnuts and cinnamon sugar. Top with other halves, pressing gently so they stick together.

Whoopie pies will keep in the refrigerator for up to 5 days, but allow them to come to room temperature before serving. Enjoy!

CHEF'S NOTE: *You can find cinnamon sugar in the baking aisle. If you'd like to make your own, mix 1 cup of granulated sugar with 2 tablespoons of cinnamon and store with your spices.*

CREAM CHEESE FROSTING

MAKES 3 CUPS

8 tablespoons salted butter, at room temperature

8 ounces cream cheese, at room temperature

3 cups powdered sugar

1 teaspoon vanilla extract

Pinch of iodized salt

Whip butter on high speed with a hand mixer or stand mixer fitted with the paddle attachment until light and fluffy, about 3 to 5 minutes.

Add cream cheese and continue whipping until no chunks remain, about 3 minutes, scraping down the sides of the bowl halfway through.

Add powdered sugar, vanilla extract, and salt. Whip until fully incorporated, 3 more minutes.

Refrigerate for at least 1 hour or until ready to use.

This frosting will keep in a sealed container in the refrigerator for 1 week.

MINT

WE HAVE been growing our mint for so long, we aren't even sure what variety it is anymore. Tall and grass-green, it seems similar to Kentucky Colonel, marking it as a prime specimen for juleps and similar beverages. Its serrated leaves stand opposite each other along the length of a square stem. The vigorous spreader also sports a soft purple flower in mid-summer, a delight for the honeybees.

This perennial heirloom crop has had many homes on the farm. In the 1960s and 1970s, the mint crept along the back of the farmstand. When the field crew passed through the doors on their way into the stand, the fresh scent would waft in with them. If a customer wanted a bunch, someone could simply lean out the back of the stand and gather it through the door. When Al went to tear down the stand in 1980, among Ferdinand's many complaints was "where will you put the mint?!" We successfully replanted it in a quiet corner of the field between Brookside Road and the end of the parking lot, where it flourished for years.

In 2007, however, we almost lost the crop entirely. When we expanded the greenhouse that year, we also extended the parking lot into the field and had to find a new home for the mint yet again. We dug it up and moved it to the slopes across the field, below the blueberry hill. There was so much mint that many of the workers took cuttings home, thinking that it would thrive anywhere. Not this variety, apparently. It withered on the rocky edge of the blueberry hill and we lost the whole crop.

Over the next season, we tried in vain to find a replacement. The sprigs we tested were too soft, too peppery, or just not strong enough. Fortunately, crewmember Christina Cocci had successfully established some of the cuttings at her home and she brought us a handful of them. We transplanted these cuttings into a familiar corner along Brookside Road where Ferdinand's favorite mint has returned to its former glory.

SOUTHSIDE

Tim Grejtak

This cocktail recipe comes from Tim Grejtak, our family friend, chemical engineer, and serious cocktail enthusiast. A few years back, while on vacation with him, we brought a case of limes and a couple bags full of our mint. This was the first thing he whipped up. We are now convinced that our mint is the only reason he calls us in the spring and summer.

According to Tim, mint's flavor comes from fine hairs on the underside of the leaf, not the leaf itself. When you muddle mint, you release the flavors from these fine hairs. You also break the leaf, releasing the enzyme chlorophyllase, which is activated by warm, acidic environments and breaks down chlorophyll, producing a swampy taste.

In a mere three shakes, this drink gives you the minty flavor without that unappealing after-taste. The first shake extracts the mint flavor, the second shake cools the mint and deactivates the chlorophyllase, and the third shake incorporates the lime juice and chills the cocktail.

Both the "up" and "fizz" variations of this cocktail are very good, but the fizz is a lighter, more refreshing drink—perfect for a warm spring day. The quality of mint is absolutely crucial for a satisfyingly minty Southside, so reach for the homegrown whenever possible.

MAKES 1 DRINK

8 sprigs mint,
plus 1 for garnish

2 ounces gin

¾ ounce simple syrup

1 ounce lime juice

Soda water (optional)

Start by muddling 8 sprigs of mint in the bottom of a cocktail shaker. Add gin and simple syrup, cover, and shake for 15 seconds.

Add a good amount of ice cubes to the shaker, cover, and shake for another 15 seconds.

Add lime juice, cover, and shake for a final 15 seconds. Strain into a chilled cocktail glass ("up") or into a highball glass filled with ice and top with soda water ("fizz").

Garnish with a sprig of mint and smile.

Anne and Ferdinand Volante courting fountain side in Italy, 1948.

FERDINAND & ANNE

NEWTON 1948

Young Anne Volante, one of Peter and Caterina's daughters, drove through "the sticks of Needham" regularly on her way to classes at Wellesley College where she majored in art and Latin. After graduating in 1930, she also received certificates from Boston University's College of Practical Arts and Letters and the Philadelphia School of Occupational Therapy. During World War II, she was an occupational therapist for injured veterans and worked at Lovell General Hospital and Mason General Hospital. She had ambitions to teach art and a love of dance, and she enjoyed the family winters in Florida.

Back in Italy, young Ferdinand Volante, Anne's distant cousin, was hard at work on his own family's farm in Gallinaro. Ferdinand lived with his father Bernardo, his mother Maddalena, and his brothers Eugenio and Peter. Their crops were nestled in the hillsides, a short drive from Anne's father's hometown of Atina, which was just across the river Melfa. They harvested a steady supply of figs, olives, and grapes, and the farmhouse attic sagged from the weight of ripening persimmons in the fall.

In the late 1940s, Anne, her sister Rose, and their parents traveled back to Italy for an extended vacation. They also wanted to meet the Italian suitor Peter had selected for Anne. Anne, however, only had eyes for Ferdinand. They married on March 13, 1949—only a short time after they met—at his family's church in Gallinaro. The couple honeymooned for a month around southern Italy, spending every last penny Ferdinand had saved.

Anne returned to the farm in America with her parents, but Ferdinand's immigration papers took many months to come through. The newlyweds kept in touch through gifts and letters while they awaited their reunion. Anne would send soft-knit American undergarments and socks to Ferdinand, and he in turn would send gold earrings and wheels of Parmigiano to Anne. When his papers finally cleared, allowing him to leave Naples, it was October 1949.

Maddalena and Bernardo Volante, Ferdinand's parents, on their family farm in Gallinaro, Italy, 1940s.

Left: Letters from Ferdinand in Italy to Anne in America, 1949; right: Ferdinand's Italian passport, 1940s.

After arriving on American shores, Ferdinand went to work in the fields with Peter and the rest of the family. Everyone got on famously and worked together to usher in the next era of Volante Farms. After Peter's death in 1953, Ferdinand, Anne, and Margie took on the bulk of farm operations with the help of Ferdinand's brother Eugenio—affectionately called Ungie—who had joined them from Italy.

By the 1960s, the growing Volante family had to decide how it would continue the traditions Peter began. Not all of Anne's siblings were interested in farming, and the acreage around the Newton farm was selling at a premium. As a leased portion of the family's land fell to developers, it became difficult to keep the farm together at that location. Meanwhile, Ferdinand had been thinking about venturing off on his own for some time. He spent his free days driving around the countryside, investigating new parcels of land and socializing with the other farmers in the area. Although he saw some good ground in New

Hampshire, the potential for roadside traffic drew him to the fifteen sprawling acres of the Fletcher Farm in Needham. It had just a few structures then, including a modest greenhouse with a small coal-fired boiler, but Ferdinand was intrigued.

On his frequent visits to Lookout Farm in South Natick, Ferdinand would often stop by the Fletcher property and ask Arthur Fletcher to let him know when he was ready to sell. Finally, in 1962, Arthur was ready to pack up and move, and he knew his children were not going to take over the farm. He drove over to Newton and shouted out the window to Ungie, "Tell your brother I'm ready!"

Yet again, another family's decision to leave farming was a boon to the Volantes. Ferdinand, Anne, and their children Helen and Alfred (Al) moved out to the Needham farm and started expanding immediately. They repurposed most of the existing buildings at first, setting up in the Fletchers' old farmstand. Anne moved the Volante farmstand business over from

Clockwise from top left: Farmstand, 1970s; the red truck in front of the farmstand, 1963; Helen and Al, 1959; Ferdinand harvesting cabbage, 1969; the Volante family kitchen, 1960s; Ferdinand and Al (far left) hanging the sign on the corner of Central Avenue and Forest Street, 1962.

Newton. She managed it and handled the books while Ferdinand and Ungie oversaw the farming operations. Margie helped at the farm part time when she wasn't taking care of Caterina, who had suffered a stroke before the move to Needham. Payroll books from 1962 show the kids pitching in as well: Al was paid a quarter an hour at age nine, while twelve-year-old Helen earned an hourly wage of seventy-five cents.

The family brought over its most loyal workers as well as the Newton farm's equipment. They soon added more fields: one where the Wellesley Country Club now borders Brookside Road, another behind the old Kinsman's Dairy near Border Road on Nehoiden Street, as well as other plots of land around town. At various times the family farmed the old McCracken land from May Street down to Rosemary Pond, as well as fields on South Street behind the Tippett Home, and a large ten-acre parcel behind the Wheeler Estate between Charles River Street and the river.

The Volantes continued to use the old Fletcher farmstand for many years, updating it slightly along the way by adding pieces of the dismantled Newton farmstand to the existing structure. The other buildings, however, got more attention. The family updated the boiler and built an assortment of new greenhouses, hotbeds, and cold frames, making the farmstand a destination for more than just produce. Ferdinand and Anne filled the greenhouses with new varieties of plants and flowers. Margie, though partially blinded by juvenile diabetes, had an knack for decoration. She chose the flowers they would grow and sell in the greenhouse each spring and lovingly planted the surrounding gardens.

At home, Anne's approach to raising their children was based on her own youth. As an American citizen of immigrant parents, she had suffered taunts and prejudice during her own childhood. Anne was fluent in English, Italian, and German but chose not to teach her children Italian. She wanted them to be Americans first in order to spare them the ridicule she endured as a child. Ferdinand's love for his new country drove him to support his wife on this topic. Even though Ferdinand and their friends and family almost exclusively spoke Italian around the house, Al and Helen never learned it.

A view of the boiler room from behind the farm, with Forest Street ahead and North Hill to the left, 1969.

UNGIE

Ferdinand's brother Ungie is integral to the Volante Farms story. While the Volante family had a strong tradition of hard labor and tireless work, Ungie added the heart and soul. Even before he and his brothers came to America, he assumed the role of patriarch with affection and a sense of humor. Their father Bernardo had twice tried to emigrate from Italy but was turned away both times because a childhood shotgun accident had permanently maimed one of his hands. As a result, he'd soured on the country. When his children asked him to visit he reportedly said "[the United States] didn't want me then, they're not getting me now."

Ungie had taken it upon himself to secure an education for his youngest brother Peter so that he could leave the family farm and have an easier life. On his brother's behalf, he had also corresponded with Anne while Ferdinand waited to clear immigration on his way to America. He was fully invested in improving the entire generation's standard of living.

Ungie was slow to give up his ties to Gallinaro and traveled back and forth frequently before settling in Newton with his family. He worked for a time with his younger brother in Detroit and at the old Newton farm with Ferdinand and Peter. Shortly after Ferdinand's father-in-law passed away, Ungie was back at the Newton farm full time. Ungie devoted the majority of his time to making the family farm in America a success.

Ungie was pure muscle and energy. When the sun came up, all the latches and doors that were closed for the night would swing free in Ungie's wake. With a mischievous glint in his eye, Ungie attacked farm life like a cyclone. If someone needed a tool, he would build it. Sticks, wires, and chunks of metal sit in the corner of the barn to this day, relics of Ungie's design. Once Ungie was semi-retired in his seventies, he returned to Gallinaro every summer. He loved fine Italian cheese and was often retrieved at the airport with a suitcase full of cheese wheels, unhappy about the customs situation.

In 1963, Ferdinand started the tradition of the farm's Christmas season, selling wreaths and trees. After a few years he got tired of the winter work and longed for a break after the harvest season. By 1967, Ungie had fully taken over the Christmas tree business. Ungie was helped every year by his son Bernie and Bernie's wife, Wendy, who was often decked out in her December miniskirt. By the time Al was studying at Babson College in 1970, he was involved in running the Christmas operations too. Once classes ended at four o'clock, he rushed home to take over the cold night shift from Ungie.

Left to right: Ferdinand and Ungie in the greenhouse, 1981; Ungie harvesting onions, 1969.

Clockwise from top: Anne and Ferdinand, 1980s; Ungie watering the cucumbers, 1970s; the farm at Christmas, 1960s; the Volante brothers: Ungie, Ferdinand, and Peter, 1990s; Ungie with his machete, 1990s.

SUMMER

AS THE DAYS grow longer and warmer, the delicious beans, corn, blueberries, and tomatoes of midsummer start to ripen. The fields are bursting by the middle of July, and the crew's focus switches from planting to harvesting. Additional hours of daylight are invested in pulling the weeds that compete for critical nutrients and monitoring rainfall forecasts for thirsty crops. Soon after the Fourth of July, the homegrown flavors of more than one hundred different varieties of vegetables overtake our shelves. As summer progresses, the perfume of local peaches and nectarines greets customers as they enter the farmstand.

Summer Recipes

FARM KITCHEN VINEGARS & VINAIGRETTES

ROASTED GARLIC

FLAP STEAK SALAD

HEIRLOOM CAPRESE SALAD

KOHLRABI SLAW

PICKLED GINGER

ESCAROLE SALAD *with* GRILLED PEACHES

GREEN BEAN SALAD *with* POTATOES

ROMESCO SAUCE

THREE BEAN SALAD

SUNGOLD TOMATO PASTA SALAD

KALE *and* QUINOA SALAD

GAZPACHO

ROASTED BEET HUMMUS ~ SMOKY EGGPLANT DIP

TOMATO BRAISED ROMANO BEANS

ASIAN PICKLED SUMMER SQUASH

SUMMER VEGETABLE PASTA ~ ARUGULA PESTO

GRILLED POLENTA *with* SUMMER VEGETABLES

HEIRLOOM TOMATO MARINARA

PAPA FERDINAND'S BOLOGNESE

PAD THAI

GRILLED CHICKEN *with* SOUTHERN STYLE BEANS

GRILLED OKRA *and* GREEN TOMATO RELISH

VEGETABLE FRIED CAULIFLOWER RICE ~ CHAR SUI PORK

INDIAN SPICED CHICKEN *with* TOMATO CHUTNEY

PEACH POLENTA UPSIDE-DOWN CAKE

CHOCOLATE ZUCCHINI CAKE

LAVENDER SUGAR COOKIES

BELLINI

FARM KITCHEN VINEGARS

Infusing vinegar with herbs and fruit is an easy way to add unexpected flavors to salad dressings and vinaigrettes. In the farm kitchen, we use just about everything—from nasturtium flowers to beautiful Thai basil. Here's a collection of some of our favorite summer flavors—but be creative! The possibilities are endless. These vinegars will keep in the refrigerator for up to 6 months.

EACH RECIPE MAKES 2 CUPS

NASTURTIUM VINEGAR

1 cup nasturtium flowers

2 cups white wine vinegar

Place nasturtium flowers in a jar and pour vinegar over top. Cover and let steep in the refrigerator for 3 to 4 weeks. Strain and discard flowers.

PURPLE BASIL VINEGAR

1 cup purple basil leaves

2 cups white balsamic vinegar

Place basil leaves in a jar and pour vinegar over top. Cover and let steep in the refrigerator for 3 to 4 weeks. Strain and discard leaves.

THAI BASIL VINEGAR

1 cup Thai basil leaves

2 cups rice vinegar

Place Thai basil leaves in a jar and pour vinegar over top. Cover and let steep in the refrigerator for 3 to 4 weeks. Strain and discard leaves.

ROASTED PEACH VINEGAR

1 to 2 slightly overripe peaches (about ¾ pound)

2 cups white wine vinegar

Preheat oven to 350°F.

Roast peaches in an ovenproof pan until they blister and soften, about 10 to 15 minutes.

Transfer peaches and any juices from the pan into a jar and pour vinegar over top. Cover and let steep in the refrigerator for 4 to 6 weeks. Strain and discard peaches.

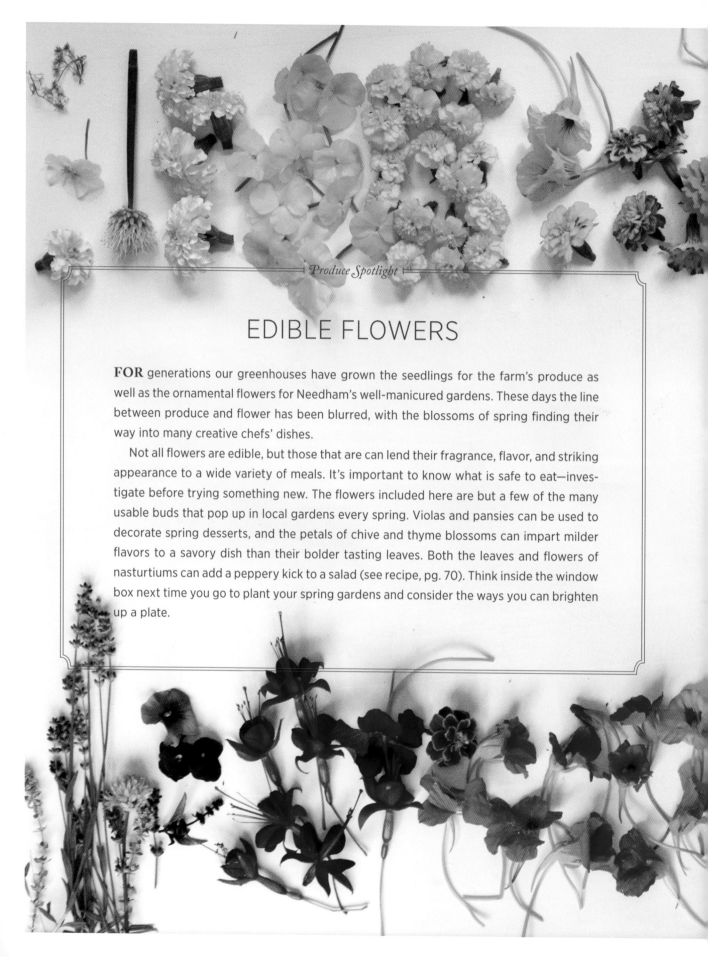

EDIBLE FLOWERS

FOR generations our greenhouses have grown the seedlings for the farm's produce as well as the ornamental flowers for Needham's well-manicured gardens. These days the line between produce and flower has been blurred, with the blossoms of spring finding their way into many creative chefs' dishes.

Not all flowers are edible, but those that are can lend their fragrance, flavor, and striking appearance to a wide variety of meals. It's important to know what is safe to eat—investigate before trying something new. The flowers included here are but a few of the many usable buds that pop up in local gardens every spring. Violas and pansies can be used to decorate spring desserts, and the petals of chive and thyme blossoms can impart milder flavors to a savory dish than their bolder tasting leaves. Both the leaves and flowers of nasturtiums can add a peppery kick to a salad (see recipe, pg. 70). Think inside the window box next time you go to plant your spring gardens and consider the ways you can brighten up a plate.

LETTUCE

TOO often relegated to the bottom of a salad bowl, our lettuce inspires such pride that we want it to rise to the top. The farm grows nineteen varieties of lettuce throughout the season—and what we grow depends upon weather conditions and the temperature tolerances of the different varieties.

We plant thirteen lettuce crops a year, one every few weeks. The seedlings germinate in the greenhouse and move to the field a couple weeks later. The heads start to fill out in about a month. Each planting will have around three thousand heads in it, which we will harvest almost entirely before moving on to the next crop.

Harvesting lettuce is a precise process. Peeling away brown and soft leaves, inspecting for rot, and keeping an eye out for goose, insect, or deer damage slows the pace just enough to allow the crew to enjoy each other's company. After the harvest, the crew brings crates bursting with green and red leaves to the stand and washes them before setting them out for sale.

Unique varieties, like Flashy Trout Back, and frilly oak-leaf types, like Panisse and Rouxai, allow us to incorporate real personality into our salads. Ferdinand loved the texture and sweetness of the delicate Buttercrunch for a small salad; Chef Todd prefers the magenta leaves of Red Sails for sandwiches; and the deli team craves the hearty Green Forest Romaine in the early spring for Caesar salads.

NASTURTIUM VINAIGRETTE

MAKES 2 CUPS

½ cup Nasturtium Vinegar
(pg. 66)

1 teaspoon Roasted Garlic

1 tablespoon Dijon mustard

1 tablespoon honey

Pinch of kosher salt

Pinch of black pepper

1¾ cups extra virgin olive oil

1 tablespoon chopped basil

1 tablespoon chopped
marjoram

In a small bowl, whisk together Nasturtium Vinegar, Roasted Garlic, mustard, honey, salt, and pepper.

While continuing to whisk, slowly add olive oil until combined.

Add chopped herbs and give mixture one final whisk.

This vinaigrette will keep in the refrigerator for 2 weeks.

ROASTED GARLIC

Roasted garlic is one of life's simple pleasures. Keep it on hand to spread across toasted bread or to mix into dishes as you're cooking. You'll find it invaluable in your kitchen—use it for sautéing and in dressings and marinades.

MAKES ½ CUP

½ cup olive oil

1 head garlic, peeled

Preheat oven to 350°F.

Submerge garlic in the olive oil in a small, ovenproof pan. Roast until golden, about 20 to 25 minutes.

Let cool and store garlic in olive oil.

Roasted Garlic will keep in the refrigerator for up to 2 weeks.

FLAP STEAK SALAD

Flap sirloin is a bit of an oddball cut that chefs prize for its high flavor-to-dollar ratio. It takes well to marinades, much like a flank steak does, but it eats like sirloin. The best of both worlds, if you ask us.

This recipe calls for Sungold tomatoes, which are incredibly sweet, orange cherry tomatoes. We use these tomatoes whenever we can, but if you cannot find them, feel free to substitute grape tomatoes.

SERVES 4 TO 6

2 pounds flap sirloin steak

2 cups Nasturtium Vinaigrette, divided

1 medium red onion, thinly sliced

1 pint grape or Sungold tomatoes

Kosher salt, to taste

Black pepper, to taste

½ pound wax beans, trimmed and halved

6 ounces baby spinach

6 ounces baby arugula

⅓ cup chopped Kalamata olives

⅓ pound high-quality blue cheese (such as Great Hill Blue or Berkshire Blue)

Marinate steak in 1 cup Nasturtium Vinaigrette for 4 to 12 hours.

Preheat oven to 375°F.

Remove steak from marinade and let sit at room temperature for about 20 minutes.

In a bowl, mix together onions, tomatoes, and a pinch of salt and pepper. Lightly coat the onions and tomatoes with ⅓ cup Nasturtium Vinaigrette. Spread on a sheet pan and roast in the oven for 15 to 18 minutes. Remove from oven and let cool.

Fill a bowl with ice water and set aside. Bring a pot of salted water to a boil. Drop wax beans into the boiling water and cook until just tender, about 2 to 3 minutes. Strain the beans and immediately submerge into the bowl of ice water. Drain and set aside.

Preheat grill to high. Grill steak to desired doneness and allow to rest for 5 to 8 minutes before slicing.

While steak is resting, assemble salad. In a large bowl, mix together spinach, arugula, roasted onions and tomatoes, olives, blue cheese, beans, and about ½ cup Nasturtium Vinaigrette (enough to coat the salad plus more to taste). Season to taste with salt and pepper.

Arrange salad on plates, slice steak, and place steak on top of greens. Serve with crusty bread.

PURPLE BASIL VINAIGRETTE

MAKES 2 CUPS

½ cup Purple Basil Vinegar
(pg. 66)

1½ teaspoons Dijon mustard

Pinch of kosher salt

Pinch of black pepper

1½ cups extra virgin olive oil

In a bowl, whisk together Purple Basil Vinegar, mustard, salt, and pepper.

While continuing to whisk, slowly add olive oil until combined.

This vinaigrette will keep in the refrigerator for 2 weeks.

HEIRLOOM CAPRESE SALAD

SERVES 4 TO 6

1½ pounds assorted heirloom tomatoes, cut into bite-size pieces

Kosher salt, to taste

Black pepper, to taste

1 to 2 heads of your favorite lettuce, chopped

1 pound mozzarella, cut into bite-size pieces

4 cups Italian bread, cut into bite-size pieces

¾ cup Purple Basil Vinaigrette

Let cut tomatoes sit in a colander for 10 minutes to drain excess juice. Season lightly with salt and pepper.

Place lettuce onto a platter and top with tomatoes, cheese, and bread. Drizzle with Purple Basil Vinaigrette and enjoy family style.

KOHLRABI SLAW

⅓ cup Roasted Peach Vinegar (pg. 66) or cider vinegar

1 tablespoon extra virgin olive oil

1½ tablespoons Beer Mustard (pg. 231) or whole grain mustard

2 tablespoons honey

1 medium kohlrabi, peeled and sliced into matchsticks

¼ head green cabbage (about ½ pound), thinly sliced

1 medium carrot, peeled and shredded

4 radishes, thinly sliced

1 cup chopped scallions

2 tablespoons chopped basil

2 tablespoons chopped parsley

Kosher salt, to taste

Black pepper, to taste

In a large bowl whisk together vinegar, olive oil, mustard, and honey.

Fold in the kohlrabi, cabbage, carrots, radishes, scallions, basil, and parsley. Season to taste with salt and pepper.

ROASTED PEACH VINAIGRETTE

½ cup Roasted Peach Vinegar (pg. 66)

1 tablespoon honey

1½ teaspoons whole grain mustard

Pinch of kosher salt

Pinch of black pepper

1½ cups extra virgin olive oil

In a bowl, whisk together the Roasted Peach Vinegar, honey, mustard, salt, and pepper.

While continuing to whisk, slowly add olive oil until combined.

This vinaigrette will keep in the refrigerator for 4 weeks.

THAI BASIL VINAIGRETTE

½ cup Thai Basil Vinegar (pg. 66)

1 tablespoon honey

1½ teaspoons chopped Pickled Ginger

Pinch of kosher salt

Pinch of black pepper

1½ cups extra virgin olive oil

In a bowl, whisk together Thai Basil Vinegar, honey, Pickled Ginger, salt, and pepper.

While continuing to whisk, slowly add olive oil until combined.

This vinaigrette will keep in the refrigerator for 4 weeks.

PICKLED GINGER

¼ pound ginger, peeled and thinly sliced

4 cups rice vinegar

3 cups water

3 tablespoons granulated sugar

1½ tablespoons kosher salt

2 pieces star anise

1 tablespoon pickling spice

1 teaspoon Szechuan peppercorns

Place ginger in a 2-quart jar or container.

Place remaining ingredients in a small pot and bring to a boil. Reduce heat and simmer for 5 minutes. Let cool completely and pour over ginger.

Cover and refrigerate for at least 2 to 4 days.

This pickled ginger will keep in the refrigerator for 6 to 8 months.

ESCAROLE SALAD *with* GRILLED PEACHES

SERVES 4 TO 6

**4 ripe peaches
(about 1¼ pounds)**

**½ cup Thai Basil Vinaigrette,
divided (pg. 75)**

Kosher salt, to taste

Black pepper, to taste

⅓ pound wax beans, trimmed

½ small red onion, diced

**1 head escarole (about 1
pound), chopped**

**⅓ cup chopped Marcona
almonds**

**6 ounces hard aged
goat cheese (we love
Midnight Moon)**

Preheat grill to high heat.

Cut peaches in half and discard pits. Lightly coat peaches with 3 tablespoons Thai Basil Vinaigrette and a pinch of salt and pepper. Grill on each side for about 4 to 5 minutes and set aside.

Lightly coat beans with 1 tablespoon Thai Basil Vinaigrette and a pinch of salt and pepper. Grill until tender, about 5 to 6 minutes, and set aside.

Cut peaches into bite-size pieces and cut beans in half. Add to a mixing bowl along with onions, escarole, and a pinch of salt and pepper.

Drizzle with remaining Thai Basil Vinaigrette and toss. Divide onto plates, sprinkle with almonds, and shave cheese on top.

Opposite page: Molly and her daughter Lisa posing with freshly picked asters, 1990s.

FIELD FLOWERS

The farm's flower arrangements have always been done first thing in the morning, while the day is still as cool and dewy as possible. When I started working at the farm in 1977, we grew three types of flowers: gladiolas, zinnias, and a few asters. Though they seem old fashioned—"midcentury"— now, gladiolas were the primary flower then. People probably paid more for a bunch of gladiolas than almost anything else we sold. There was an art to cutting them at just the right moment, especially in hot weather. They had to show color, but not too much. Zinnias and asters were made into bunches of ten to twelve stems. We'd walk down a row, cutting the open flowers, then tying off a bunch when we had the right count. The bunches were rested on top of the plants then collected gently in a bushel basket when we got to the end of a row. It was all about working quickly. If every open zinnia was pink, that was the bouquet. To mix them more mindfully would have been too much of a luxury—we had to get back inside and open up the stand!

Back then we used field knives to cut the flowers; I cut my thumb all the time. By the early 1980s, we had stopped growing gladiolas—they were less popular and too much work. Zinnias and asters remained in demand. We always sold out, but we couldn't spare the hours to cut more. We were in the "new" stand by then, and it was much bigger and busier.

Ferdinand Volante's friend Carmine Socci began making bouquets at the farm in the late 1980s. He came in several days a week and arranged the bouquets. It really helped the supply catch up with the demand. He incorporated a greater variety of flowers into the bouquets, like black-eyed Susans, and the bunches were larger.

Around 1991, this job reverted to the Volante staff, and a specific area was designated for "bunching." There was room in a large new chest to keep flowers cool when they came in from the field. Early in the day, we cut a variety of blossoms, then we mixed them into bunches back in the farmstand. This way, we had more time to create bouquets that really showcased them.

Other notable improvements that allowed us to develop this crop included the use of clippers.

Why do we love flowers? A single flower can sanctify a space, infuse a room with fragrance, provide a focal point, and lighten a dark mood. They are a source of admirable color—vivid or soft. Their rays, rings, stars, and spirals are geometrical wonders of structure. They are a sign of life and fertility. Many of the things we grow at the farm are brought forth from flowers; bees and pollination are essential to food production. May they bloom on!

-Molly Lyne, manager,
Volante Farms 1977 to 2002

GREEN BEAN SALAD *with* POTATOES

SERVES 4 TO 6

3 to 4 red potatoes (about ½ pound)

Kosher salt, to taste

1 pound green beans, trimmed

¼ head red cabbage (about ½ pound), thinly sliced

1 14-ounce can garbanzo beans, drained and rinsed

1 tablespoon chopped fresh savory

1 cup chopped scallions

1½ cups Romesco Vinaigrette

Black pepper, to taste

1 head red Boston lettuce, chopped

Place potatoes in a medium pot and add just enough water to cover them. Add a pinch of salt. Bring to a boil, then simmer until just tender, about 15 to 20 minutes. Drain and rinse with cold water. Pat dry and set aside.

Fill a bowl with ice water and set aside. Bring a pot of salted water to a boil. Drop beans into the water and cook until just tender, about 3 to 5 minutes. Strain beans and immediately submerge into the bowl of ice water.

Drop red cabbage into boiling water and cook until just tender, about 1 minute. Strain cabbage and immediately submerge into the bowl of ice water with beans. When cool, strain beans and cabbage and pat dry. Set aside.

Cut potatoes into bite-size pieces. Place in a bowl and add beans, cabbage, garbanzo beans, savory, scallions, and Romesco Vinaigrette. Toss to combine and season to taste with salt and pepper. Divide lettuce onto plates and top with green bean mixture.

ROMESCO VINAIGRETTE

MAKES 2 CUPS

⅔ cup Romesco Sauce

¼ cup sherry vinegar

2 tablespoons water

Pinch of kosher salt

Pinch of black pepper

1 cup extra virgin olive oil

In a bowl, whisk together Romesco Sauce, vinegar, water, and a pinch of salt and pepper.

While continuing to whisk, slowly add olive oil until combined.

This vinaigrette will keep in the refrigerator for 1 week.

ROMESCO SAUCE

Romesco is a pepper and nut purée originating from the Catalonia region of Spain. It's a rich and smoky sauce that will enhance pretty much any dish. (Of course, no one will stop you if you just eat it with fresh, crusty bread.) In our version, that irresistible smoky flavor is supplied by the charred bell pepper, ancho chile, and smoked paprika—but don't be fooled. Those toasted hazelnuts and almonds do a lot of work here, too.

MAKES 2 CUPS

1 red bell pepper, halved and deseeded

¾ cup extra virgin olive oil, divided

Kosher salt, to taste

Black pepper, to taste

1 thick slice crusty bread

1 tablespoon chopped garlic

1 dried ancho chile, stem removed

1 pound assorted ripe tomatoes, cored and halved

3 tablespoons sherry vinegar

¼ cup sliced toasted almonds

¼ cup toasted hazelnuts

1½ tablespoons chopped parsley

1 teaspoon smoked paprika

1 tablespoon lemon juice

Preheat oven to 375°F.

Mix together the bell pepper, ½ tablespoon olive oil, and a pinch of salt and pepper. Roast on a sheet pan until the skin starts to blister, about 15 to 20 minutes. Remove from oven, let cool, and remove skin.

Heat 2 tablespoons olive oil in a sauté pan over medium heat. Add bread and brown each side. Remove and set aside. Add 1 tablespoon olive oil to pan. Add garlic and ancho chile and cook for about 30 seconds. Add the tomatoes, vinegar, and a pinch of salt and pepper. Reduce heat and simmer for 15 minutes. Remove from heat and let cool.

Add almonds to a food processor and pulse until ground but not powdery. Remove almonds, add hazelnuts, and repeat process.

Return almonds to food processor along with tomato mixture, bell pepper, remaining olive oil (about ½ cup), parsley, paprika, lemon juice, and a pinch of salt and pepper. Crumble bread by hand and add to food processor. Pulse until incorporated, about 30 to 45 seconds. Season to taste with salt and pepper. Serve as a dip with crusty bread, mix into hummus, or slather on a sandwich.

BEANS

FOR many years, we grew just a few types of beans, chief among them the Spartan Arrow. This big green bean was a favorite of the field crew as it filled a bushel quickly and was easy to pick. But alas, in the early 2000s, we lost this variety and began the search for its replacement. In an effort to find a substitute, we introduced a host of new beans to our customers and sought their feedback. Instead of finding a solitary favorite, our customers embraced the diverse offerings, and as a result, we decided to keep them.

Now it is not unusual for the farmstand to offer five or more types of green beans on a given day. Beyond green, there is a kaleidoscope of other beans our customers count on. Yellow wax beans have a solid following. The incredibly popular flat Romano beans keep people coming back for more—especially our Italian customers. Late-season pink and white mottled shell beans are perfect for soups or for rounding out a three-bean salad. The lima is perhaps the most maligned and underestimated bean around; nothing like the frozen and canned versions of schoolhouse nightmares, our field fresh limas can be transcendental in a summer succotash.

THREE BEAN SALAD

⅓ pound green beans, trimmed

⅓ pound wax beans, trimmed

⅓ pound Romano beans, trimmed

¼ head red cabbage (about ½ pound), thinly sliced

1 tablespoon Dijon mustard

3 tablespoons red wine vinegar

Kosher salt, to taste

Black pepper, to taste

⅓ cup extra virgin olive oil

4 radishes, sliced

1 medium cucumber, thinly sliced

½ pint grape or Sungold tomatoes, halved

1 cup chopped scallions

1 tablespoon chopped parsley

1 tablespoon chopped dill

Fill a bowl with ice water and set aside. Bring a pot of salted water to a boil. Drop green beans into the water and cook until just tender, about 2 to 3 minutes. Strain the beans and immediately submerge into the bowl of ice water. Repeat this process with the wax beans and Romano beans. The Romano beans will require 1 to 2 additional minutes of cooking time. Refresh the ice water bowl as needed.

With the pot of salted water still boiling, drop the cabbage in and cook for 30 seconds. Strain the cabbage and immediately submerge into the bowl of ice water.

Once cool, drain the beans and cabbage and pat dry. In a large bowl, whisk together the mustard, vinegar, and a pinch of salt and pepper.

While continuing to whisk, slowly add olive oil until combined.

Add all remaining ingredients, beans, and cabbage and mix thoroughly. Season to taste with salt and pepper.

Enjoy chilled or at room temperature as a delicious side dish.

SUNGOLD TOMATO PASTA SALAD

1 pound bowtie pasta

½ cup pitted black olives, chopped

1 cup quartered artichoke hearts, store bought

½ cup feta cheese, crumbled

8 ounces spinach

1 cup chopped basil

2 cups Sungold Vinaigrette

Kosher salt, to taste

Black pepper, to taste

Cook pasta according to package instructions, let cool, and set aside.

In a large bowl, mix together pasta, olives, artichoke hearts, feta, spinach, basil, and Sungold Vinaigrette. Season to taste with salt and pepper and serve cold or at room temperature.

SUNGOLD VINAIGRETTE

1 cup extra virgin olive oil, divided

1 tablespoon minced garlic

½ pint Sungold tomatoes

¼ cup white balsamic vinegar

1 tablespoon chopped oregano leaves

Pinch of kosher salt

Pinch of black pepper

Heat 2 tablespoons olive oil in a large sauté pan over medium-high heat. Add garlic and cook until fragrant and beginning to brown, about 20 seconds. Add tomatoes and lower heat to medium. Cook tomatoes until their skins break, about 8 to 10 minutes. Remove from heat and add vinegar. Transfer to a bowl and let cool.

Whisk in oregano and a pinch of salt and pepper.

While continuing to whisk, slowly add remaining olive oil until combined.

This vinaigrette will keep in the refrigerator for 1 week.

KALE *and* QUINOA SALAD

This recipe calls for Delfino cilantro, a feathery looking variety, with all the bright notes of traditional cilantro, but somehow milder. It pairs wonderfully with this vinaigrette.

SERVES 4 TO 6

1½ cups quinoa

Kosher salt, to taste

1 bunch kale, thinly sliced (about 4 cups)

1 red bell pepper, diced

1 cup chopped scallions

3 radishes, thinly sliced

2 tablespoons chopped Delfino cilantro

1½ cups Corn and Holy Mole Pepper Vinaigrette (pg. 90)

Black pepper, to taste

Place quinoa in a pot with 2½ cups of water, add a pinch of salt, and bring to a boil. Once boiling, reduce to a simmer and cook until quinoa is tender, about 10 to 15 minutes. Add kale and cook for 2 more minutes. Strain the quinoa and kale and let cool completely.

In a large bowl, mix the quinoa and kale with the bell pepper, scallions, radishes, and cilantro. Add the Corn and Holy Mole Pepper Vinaigrette and mix again. Season to taste with salt and pepper.

Serve cold or at room temperature.

CORN *and* HOLY MOLE PEPPER VINAIGRETTE

MAKES 3 CUPS

1 holy mole pepper (or poblano pepper), stem removed

1¼ cups extra virgin olive oil, divided

2 ears corn

Kosher salt, to taste

Black pepper, to taste

3 tablespoons white wine vinegar

2 tablespoons lime juice

¼ teaspoon smoked paprika

Preheat oven to 400°F.

Lightly coat the pepper with ½ teaspoon olive oil and place on a sheet pan. Remove the corn husks and lightly coat the cobs with 1 tablespoon olive oil and a pinch of salt and pepper. Place on the sheet pan with the pepper.

Cook in oven for 12 minutes, then remove corn. Continue cooking pepper until it flattens and the skin becomes loose, an additional 5 to 10 minutes. Remove from oven and let cool.

Cut corn off cob and place into blender. Remove and discard skin and seeds from the pepper. Add pepper to blender and purée for 30 seconds. Add vinegar, lime juice, paprika, and a pinch of salt and pepper and pulse for 10 seconds.

With blender on lowest setting, slowly add remaining olive oil (about 1 cup) until fully combined. Season to taste with salt and pepper.

CUCUMBERS

CUCUMBERS are critical to the farm. We grow two summer crops in the field and a spring and fall crop in the greenhouse. Pickling cucumbers are firm and sized to fit in a jar, maxing out around six inches. Though pickling seems like an end-of-season activity, these perfect-for-pickling cucumbers peak in July. Our slicing cucumber is Marketmore 76, which we have grown for decades. They—and the rest of the cucumbers—have a central role at Volante family meal times. Al considers a cucumber and tomato sandwich key to a complete day, but his son Steve holds the real family recipe. He hollows out the center of a large cucumber by cutting off one end and boring it out with a field knife. He then stuffs it chock full of crushed ice and enjoys.

THE HISTORY OF THE NEEDHAM FARMLAND

THE fifteen acres at the corner of Central Avenue and Forest Street in Needham have been continuously farmed for more than three centuries. In 1774, wealthy Dedham landowner Deacon Woodcock let his grandson, Jeremiah Woodcock Jr., build the first home on the property, which he moved into following the Revolutionary War. Jeremiah's brother Samuel built the barn tucked into the woods on Brookside Road. The land stayed in the Woodcock family well into the 1800s. After that, the farm traded hands several times as various families tried to make a go of farming it, until Lucy Fletcher purchased the land in 1927. Lucy and her husband Arthur farmed this land until 1962, when Ferdinand Volante moved with his family to Needham. Lucy Fletcher's granddaughter, Linda Mauro, spent her early childhood on the farm and still works here.

Opposite page, clockwise from top left: The Jeremiah Woodcock House on Brookside Road was the original home on this farmland, built in 1774; an order form from Arthur Fletcher's farm, 1930s; Arthur Fletcher watering in his greenhouse, 1950s; wooden dibble(r)s, our traditional tool for making holes in soil flats for transplanting seedlings.

A. W. FLETCHER'S
CENTRAL AVENUE NURSERY

829 Central Avenue,   Needham, Mass.
Telephone   Needham 0048

_____ 193___

Sold To _____

Monday 8 A. M. 8

10 _Ford June Gris._
10 _Canstee   "   Pink_

IN the early years, workhorses plowed the fields before the arrival of a Farmall tractor. The fields and cart road, located next to the current greenhouse, appear today just as they did back then. Brookside Road was a packed dirt road with many large trees on both sides shading its path.

The farmstand was a seasonal business. Farm preparation started around January each year. My grandparents spent winters tending to maintenance in the greenhouse and ordering seeds. Many of the original seed companies they used, such as Harris, Ball, and W. Atlee Burpee & Co., are still in business, providing seeds to Volante Farms today. A few loyal workers joined their two daughters and older grandchildren to help in the farmstand and the fields. The main greenhouse was heated by coal, and it was where seedlings were transplanted into small wooden boxes with tar paper separators, twelve to a box. Wooden dibbles were used to make the holes in the soil when transplanting, just as they are today.

Pansies, strawberries, and peas were the main spring crops. Back then, pansies were grown in the field, and customers were allowed to choose the plants they wanted. Once chosen, the plant was dug up and placed into an individual box. If you wanted a particular variety of tomato, you could choose it from a cold frame and take it home wrapped in newspaper for a quick transplant. Corn in the 1950s was fifty cents per dozen, and the excess bushels of corn were taken into Boston to sell in the mornings. With no cash registers in the farmstand, sales were figured on a brown paper bag or small pad of paper, so math skills were as necessary in those days as computer skills are today. My family still has fond memories of using a hand pump that was attached to a well in the back of the old greenhouse. On hot summer days, we drank the cool, clear water it provided using a tin cup that hung nearby.

-Linda Mauro, manager, Volante Farms, 2003 to present

GAZPACHO

We make this gazpacho every year during peak tomato season when we have an abundance of heirlooms. While you can make this recipe easily using single variety garden tomatoes, it is the combination of assorted heirlooms and Sungolds that gives this dish its tremendous depth.

MAKES ABOUT 8 CUPS

1 pint Sungold tomatoes

4 pounds heirloom tomatoes (a variety is best)

2 cucumbers (about 1 pound), peeled and deseeded

1 small red onion

1 green bell pepper, deseeded

1 red bell pepper, deseeded

1 tablespoon kosher salt, plus more to taste

½ teaspoon black pepper, plus more to taste

2 tablespoons sherry vinegar

2 tablespoons orange juice

1 tablespoon lime juice

2 tablespoons extra virgin olive oil

Splash of your favorite hot sauce (optional)

Slice the Sungolds in half and set aside. Core and quarter the remaining tomatoes, then squeeze them over a strainer set in a bowl to remove the seeds. Discard the seeds, then save and set aside the tomatoes and their juices.

Roughly chop the cucumbers, onion, and peppers.

Working in batches, add half of the cucumbers, onions, and peppers to a blender and pulse for 15 seconds. Add half of the tomatoes and tomato juice. Purée until smooth (some small chunks are okay), about 45 seconds, and pour puréed mixture into a bowl. Repeat with remaining vegetables, add salt and pepper, and combine in the bowl.

Stir in remaining ingredients and season to taste with salt and pepper. Add a splash of hot sauce if you desire.

Serve cold as a summer appetizer.

ROASTED BEET HUMMUS

2 beets (about 1 pound), rinsed and greens discarded

3 tablespoons extra virgin olive oil, divided

2 teaspoons za'atar, divided

Kosher salt, to taste

Black pepper, to taste

1 14-ounce can garbanzo beans, drained and rinsed

¼ cup tahini paste

2 tablespoons chopped garlic

2 tablespoons lemon juice

1 teaspoon ground cumin

Preheat oven to 400°F.

Toss beets with 1 tablespoon olive oil, 1 teaspoon za'atar, and a pinch of salt and pepper. Place on a sheet pan and cook until tender, about 45 to 60 minutes depending on their size. Remove from oven and let cool for 10 to 15 minutes.

Put garbanzo beans, tahini paste, and garlic into a food processor. Purée for 30 seconds. Add lemon juice, 1 tablespoon water, cumin, remaining za'atar, remaining olive oil, and a pinch of salt and pepper. Pulse until well combined, about 30 seconds, and scoop into a bowl.

Using a paper towel, wipe the skin off of the beets, cut them in half, and place into the food processor. Pulse until smooth, about 30 seconds. If the mixture gets too thick, add a tablespoon of water. Combine beet purée with hummus.

Season to taste with salt and pepper. Serve with pita chips or crudité, or enjoy as a sandwich spread.

SMOKY EGGPLANT DIP

MAKES 2 CUPS

2 large eggplants

Kosher salt, to taste

Black pepper, to taste

½ cup extra virgin olive oil, divided

1 medium yellow onion, diced

1 tablespoon chopped garlic

½ teaspoon anchovy paste

1 teaspoon ground cumin

1½ teaspoons smoked paprika

Pinch of chili flakes

2 teaspoons sherry vinegar

1 tablespoon chopped parsley

Preheat oven to 350°F.

Using a paring knife, pierce each eggplant all over (this will help release moisture while they cook) then lightly sprinkle with salt and pepper. Roast on a sheet pan until eggplants soften and start to deflate, about 35 to 45 minutes.

While the eggplants roast, add 2 tablespoons olive oil to a large sauté pan over medium-high heat. Add onions and cook until golden brown, about 10 to 12 minutes. Add garlic and anchovy paste and cook for 1 minute, stirring constantly. Remove from heat and add cumin, paprika, chili flakes, and vinegar. Set aside.

Remove eggplants from oven and let cool for 15 minutes.

Scoop out eggplants and roughly chop flesh, discarding the skins. Place flesh in a large bowl.

Mix together eggplant, onion mixture, and parsley. Using a traditional or immersion blender, pulse mixture, adding remaining olive oil until fully combined. Season to taste with salt and pepper.

Serve at room temperature with your favorite crackers and bread or enjoy as a sandwich spread.

TOMATO BRAISED ROMANO BEANS

Romano beans are a nice alternative to traditional green beans; they have the same bright flavor but a meatier texture. They are also robust enough to hold up in braises, which is how we're using them here. This dish is a great summer side when you're looking for something hearty but light.

SERVES 4 TO 6

2 tablespoons olive oil

1 tablespoon chopped garlic

1 pint grape or Sungold tomatoes

2 tablespoons balsamic vinegar

Kosher salt, to taste

Black pepper, to taste

1 pound Romano beans, trimmed

1 tablespoon chopped oregano leaves

Heat olive oil in a wide-bottomed pot over medium-high heat. Add garlic and cook until lightly toasted, about 30 to 45 seconds. Add tomatoes and stir so as not to burn the garlic. Cook until tomatoes start to blister, about 2 minutes.

Add the vinegar and a pinch of salt and pepper. Reduce heat to low and simmer for about 10 minutes. Crush the tomatoes slightly, breaking up any that are still intact.

Add beans, cover, and simmer until tender, about 15 to 20 minutes.

Remove from heat, add oregano, and season to taste with salt and pepper.

ASIAN PICKLED SUMMER SQUASH

This squash is delicious and beautiful—but if you want to add even more color and a spicy kick, toss a few thinly sliced radishes into the mix.

MAKES ABOUT 4 CUPS

1¼ cups rice vinegar

1 cup water

¼ cup granulated sugar

3 tablespoons kosher salt

1 tablespoon crystalized ginger

2 pieces star anise

1 sprig Thai basil

1 sprig cilantro

2 summer squash (about 1 pound), cut into spears

Add vinegar, water, sugar, salt, ginger, and star anise to a pot. Bring to a boil, then lower heat and simmer for 10 minutes. Remove from heat and let cool completely.

Squeeze the basil and cilantro by hand to lightly bruise them, then add to the brine. Place squash in a quart container and pour brine over the squash, covering it completely. Seal container and refrigerate for a few days to pickle before eating.

Pickled squash will keep in a sealed container in the refrigerator for up to 4 months.

SUMMER VEGETABLE PASTA

This is the perfect summer dish. In the farm kitchen, we cook the couscous in Corn Stock (pg. 157), which adds an immense amount of flavor and depth to this meal.

SERVES 4 TO 6

3 cups Israeli or M'Hamsa couscous

1½ cups fresh corn kernels (about 2 ears)

1 medium zucchini, cut into 1-inch dice

1 medium summer squash, cut into 1-inch dice

½ pint grape or Sungold tomatoes, halved

Kosher salt, to taste

Black pepper, to taste

2 tablespoons olive oil

⅔ cup Arugula Pesto

Cook couscous according to package instructions and set aside.

Preheat oven to 450°F with 2 sheet pans on the racks.

In a bowl, mix together corn, zucchini, squash, tomatoes, and a pinch of salt and pepper. Lightly coat the vegetables with olive oil.

Divide mixture evenly onto preheated sheet pans and cook for 5 minutes. Remove pans from oven and stir vegetables. Before returning pans to oven, make sure to spread vegetables out again. Cook until golden brown, another 8 to 10 minutes. Remove pans from oven and let cool.

Mix together couscous, vegetables, and Arugula Pesto. Season to taste with salt and pepper and enjoy hot or cold.

ARUGULA PESTO

This pesto marries the distinctive flavors of arugula and pistachios to create an exceptional pasta sauce. It's equally delicious with eggs, in soups and sandwiches, or stuffed under the skin of a whole chicken and roasted.

MAKES ABOUT 2 CUPS

½ cup grated Romano cheese

½ cup toasted pistachios

1½ teaspoons chopped garlic

8 ounces baby arugula

1 cup basil leaves

⅓ cup extra virgin olive oil

Kosher salt, to taste

Black pepper, to taste

Place cheese, pistachios, and garlic into a food processor and pulse until ground, about 20 seconds. Add the arugula, basil, olive oil, and a pinch of salt and pepper and pulse for 10 seconds. Using a rubber spatula, scrape down the sides of the bowl. Pulse for another 20 seconds until arugula is fully puréed. Season to taste with salt and pepper.

This pesto will keep in the freezer for 6 to 8 months.

GRILLED POLENTA *with* SUMMER VEGETABLES

SERVES 4 TO 6

POLENTA

1 tablespoon kosher salt, plus more to taste

1 cup coarse cornmeal

1 cup fresh corn kernels (about 1 to 2 ears)

⅓ cup freshly grated Fontina cheese

⅓ cup freshly grated Asiago cheese

2 tablespoons salted butter

Black pepper, to taste

Olive oil, for brushing

SUMMER VEGETABLES

1 medium eggplant, cut into ½-inch-thick rounds

3 tablespoons olive oil, plus more for brushing

Kosher salt, to taste

Black pepper, to taste

4 assorted bell peppers (about 3 to 4 pounds), cut into strips

1 tablespoon chopped garlic

1 tablespoon chopped capers

1 sprig rosemary

3 tablespoons red wine vinegar

¼ cup chopped basil

1 tablespoon fresh oregano

½ pound fresh mozzarella, thinly sliced

Make polenta. Bring 5 cups water and 1 tablespoon salt to a boil in a wide-bottomed pot. Slowly add cornmeal, whisking constantly. Reduce heat to low. Continue cooking, whisking occasionally to keep polenta from sticking, until it reaches a creamy texture and pulls away from the sides of the pot, about 30 to 40 minutes.

Remove from heat and stir in corn, cheeses, and butter. Season to taste with salt and pepper.

Pour polenta onto a sheet pan and spread so it is even with the top of the pan. If polenta does not fill the entire sheet pan that is okay; but take care to make sure the thickness is consistent. Refrigerate for at least 2 hours or overnight.

Preheat grill to high. Gently transfer from the pan onto a cutting board. Cut into circles and lightly brush with olive oil. Grill the pieces until they are easily freed from the grates, flip, and repeat on the opposite side. (You can grill the polenta pieces ahead of time, refrigerate them for up to 3 hours, and reheat in the oven when ready to use.)

Preheat oven to 400°F.

Prepare vegetables. Brush eggplant with olive oil and sprinkle with salt and pepper. Arrange slices on a sheet pan and roast until golden brown and tender, about 18 to 24 minutes.

Heat olive oil in a large sauté pan over medium-high heat. Add half of the peppers and cook for 6 to 8 minutes, stirring a few times. Remove peppers from pan and set aside. Repeat with second batch of peppers. When both batches are done cooking, return all peppers to the pan.

Add garlic and cook for 2 minutes. Add capers, rosemary, and vinegar and cook until vinegar completely reduces, about 4 to 5 minutes. Discard rosemary and fold in basil and oregano. Season to taste with salt and pepper.

Before assembling, make sure polenta, eggplant, and peppers are hot. If not, warm them in a 350°F oven for a few minutes.

Plate the polenta, layer on the mozzarella and eggplant, and place peppers on top.

TOMATOES

BOTH bountiful and temperamental, tomatoes require patience and skill to grow. When the weather cooperates, however, they grow so well on their own that Al has been known to exclaim, "This crop makes us look like geniuses!" We grow up to forty varieties of plums, slicers, heirlooms, and cherries every year. The plants begin as seedlings in the greenhouse in mid-March and then go into the ground in late May. We expose the seedlings to wind and cool temperatures in the open bay of the greenhouse to toughen them up before they head out to the field.

For decades, the Early Girl has been our primary red slicing tomato. This variety matures quickly and is the perfect blend of sweet and tangy. There hasn't been a tomato we've grown—and we try others all the time—that has compared to the Early Girl. We trellis about two thousand Early Girls every season. Each has a piece of twine loosely tied at its base as well as to a wire strung at about eye level. We pull the wire taut between old iron steam pipes that were once used in the sash beds that predate the modern greenhouses. The plants gain a fair amount of weight over the season, and this system usually holds up to the stress. Although it can be upsetting when it fails and the wires break, it does feel good to know we have grown a tomato that can snap metal.

We prune the plants every week or so, removing side shoots and carefully winding the twine so that it will support the clusters of fruit. Usually about two months after transplant, the first green globes that have burst from bright yellow blossoms will start to show a slight blush of red.

In recent years, the demand for heirloom tomatoes has skyrocketed, leading us to seek out more amazing varieties. While many heirlooms are beautifully hued and come in an assortment of shapes and sizes, they also tend to have cracks and so-called imperfections. Moreover, they are less productive in the field and require more space to produce fewer, though often heavier, fruit. In fact, we grow them in cages with only one plant in the space of four regular tomato plants. All is forgiven, of course, once you have a taste.

Sauce tomatoes are a different beast entirely. Finding the right one has occupied much of our time on the farm. Ferdinand had a favorite: the Socci Plum, a variety that Charlie Socci cultivated. It was Ferdinand's preferred fruit for bolognese, and even though we didn't always grow them to sell, there were always a dozen or so plants in the field for Ferdinand.

In the late 1990s, the genetics of the Socci Plum started to fade on us and we went in search of another option. We found it in Mr. Gallinelli's Plum, which remains our plum of choice both in the fields and for our customers to grow at home. Mr. Gallinelli would produce the seeds for Ferdinand every year and deliver them in mid-winter, providing plenty of time for us to sow them in the greenhouse. This fruit has held up extremely well, and now we produce our own seeds at the end of each season. We set aside a few plants that are particularly nice specimens, harvest the ripest tomatoes, and clean the seeds from them on a rainy fall day. The seeds are then set to dry for several weeks before being stored until spring. This process has worked well for maintaining the Gallinelli Plum and a few other special heirlooms we can't find elsewhere.

The tomato harvest starts light in July and picks up through August and into September. The crew harvests two or three times a week. It is a massive undertaking that strips the plants of all the fruit that is at least halfway ripe. In the truck, the crew sorts the tomatoes by ripeness, and they are sorted again at the farmstand so that the ripest are always available to the customers. In the depths of September, it is an all-day project to sort and replenish the displays in the farmstand.

HEIRLOOM TOMATO MARINARA

This is not a traditional marinara, but one born from the harvest of our farm. Caramelizing the vegetables and reducing the balsamic vinegar adds a natural sweetness, so no additional sugar is needed.

3 tablespoons olive oil

2 medium yellow onions (about 1 pound)

1 medium fennel bulb, cored and roughly chopped

2 red bell peppers (about 1½ pounds), deseeded and roughly chopped

2½ tablespoons chopped garlic

1 fresh bay leaf

3 tablespoons balsamic vinegar

3 pounds heirloom tomatoes (a variety is best)

Kosher salt, to taste

Black pepper, to taste

2 teaspoons chopped oregano leaves

⅔ cup basil leaves

Heat olive oil in a large pot or dutch oven over medium-high heat. Add onions and fennel and cook until golden brown, about 12 to 15 minutes. Add peppers and cook for 10 minutes. Add garlic and bay leaf and cook for 5 minutes. Add vinegar and simmer until almost completely reduced, about 5 minutes more.

Core and halve tomatoes, squeezing to remove seeds. Stir in tomatoes and a hearty pinch of salt and pepper. Bring to a boil, and then reduce heat to a simmer. Cook for 2 to 3 hours, stirring every so often. Your final sauce should be thick, dark, and rich.

Remove from heat and season to taste with salt and pepper. Stir in oregano and basil and let sit for 5 minutes. Pass through a food mill to get rid of tomato skins.

This marinara will keep in the refrigerator for up to 5 days and in the freezer for up to 6 months.

PAPA FERDINAND'S BOLOGNESE

When our family talks about red sauce (which is surprisingly often), we always come back to this recipe as the gold standard.

Our grandfather, Papa Ferdinand, used to make this during the summer; he'd start first thing in the morning and leave the sauce to simmer while we worked until noon. At lunch we'd often skip the pasta, instead opting for a loaf of (now defunct) Cavagni's bread to cover with the hearty sauce.

This recipe is as rustic as it gets, calling for unpeeled tomatoes, chunks of vegetables, and hunks of meat; it's filling enough to be a meal on its own.

– Steve Volante

MAKES 4 QUARTS

2 tablespoons olive oil

½ pound spicy Italian sausage

½ pound bone-in beef (such as chuck roll or short rib)

½ pound bone-in chicken (such as thigh or leg)

1 medium onion, diced

1 large carrot, peeled and diced

1 celery stalk, diced

3 tablespoons minced garlic

½ cup red wine

¼ cup balsamic vinegar

6 pounds plum tomatoes, roughly chopped

2 tablespoons tomato paste

2 cups basil

Kosher salt, to taste

Black pepper, to taste

Heat olive oil in a large stockpot over medium-high heat. Poke a couple of holes in the sausage casings and add to pot. Brown sausage on both sides, remove from pot, and set aside.

Pat dry beef and chicken and add to pot. Brown, remove, and set aside, leaving any rendered juices and fat in the pot. (Do this in batches if necessary to prevent crowding.)

Add onions, carrots, and celery to pot and cook until they begin to brown, about 5 minutes, stirring occasionally. Add garlic and cook for 1 minute. The vegetables should absorb most of the fat and olive oil in the pot so keep a close eye to prevent burning (add more olive oil if necessary). Add wine and vinegar and reduce by half, about 4 to 6 minutes.

Return beef and sausage to the pot and add tomatoes and tomato paste. Stir, bring to a low boil, then reduce heat and simmer for 1 hour, stirring occasionally.

Add chicken and simmer another 2 hours, stirring occasionally.

Add basil, season to taste with salt and pepper, and simmer another 15 minutes. Check sauce for consistency. It should be chunky and easily coat the back of a spoon. If sauce is too thin, stir in 1 or 2 more tablespoons of tomato paste.

Serve this robust masterpiece over pasta or on chunks of bread.

This bolognese will keep in the refrigerator for up to 5 days and in the freezer for up to 6 months.

DINNER IN THE FIELD

WHEN Chef Todd Heberlein joined the farm, his experience and passion for farm-to-table dining was evident and spawned our Dinner in the Field events. Each meal is an elevated gourmet journey through our humble vegetable rows. As harvested crops are sent to the kitchen, Chef Todd transforms them into a multi-course extravaganza, using as many unique varieties as possible. Each meal may offer up to ten dishes over five courses, many highlighting our local partners. Along the dirt road that traverses the main field, guests sit at cozy tables of eight with friends and new faces. The evening's rhythm is studded with sips of crisp wine and delicate cucumber-herb water as Chef Todd annotates the meal with tasting notes. Each meal closes with a sweet take on the vegetable of the moment by Chef Todd's wife, Jen, who is also our head pastry chef.

The ever-changing menu shines a light on the local food movement we foster in the community and display in the farmstand. These meals are the result of the perfect confluence of ingredients, time, and talent. They are truly labors of love from the family and staff of Volante Farms, exhibiting the pride we have in our work. Many of this book's recipes are born from past Dinners in the Field, simplified for replication in the home kitchen.

PAD THAI

1 pound rice stick noodles (or linguine)

3 tablespoons tamarind paste

2 tablespoons fish sauce

2 tablespoons honey

3 tablespoons rice wine vinegar

2 tablespoons peanut oil

2 tablespoons chopped garlic

1 cup chopped scallions

¼ head green cabbage (about ½ pound), thinly sliced

2 medium carrots (about ½ pound), shredded

2 heads baby bok choy, thinly sliced

1 medium kohlrabi, cut into matchsticks

2 eggs, beaten

Chili flakes, to taste (optional)

2 tablespoons chopped Thai basil

1 tablespoon chopped mint

1 tablespoon chopped cilantro

¼ cup chopped roasted peanuts

1 lime, cut into wedges

Cook noodles according to package instructions and set aside.

Thoroughly mix tamarind paste into ½ cup warm water. Strain tamarind-water mixture to remove any seeds. Mix together tamarind-water mixture, fish sauce, honey, and rice wine vinegar in a bowl and set aside.

Heat half the oil in a wide-bottomed pot over medium-high heat. Add half the garlic and scallions and cook for 30 seconds. Add half the cabbage, carrots, bok choy, and kohlrabi and cook for 1 minute. Set aside and repeat the process with the other half of the vegetables. When the second half is cooked, return the first batch to the pot.

Push vegetables to the sides of the pot and add eggs to the center. Scramble eggs until almost cooked, about 30 seconds.

Mix in reserved noodles and sauce and cook for 1 minute more. Remove from heat. Add chili flakes if desired.

Divide onto plates and garnish with Thai basil, mint, cilantro, peanuts, and lime wedges.

GRILLED CHICKEN *with* SOUTHERN STYLE BEANS

SERVES 6

CHICKEN

2 tablespoons chopped
Delfino cilantro

3 tablespoons Dijon mustard

2 tablespoons chopped garlic

3 tablespoons honey

⅓ cup lime juice

¼ cup olive oil

⅓ cup soy sauce

Pinch of black pepper

6 chicken legs

BEANS

2 tablespoons olive oil

¼ cup diced bacon

1 medium yellow onion,
thinly sliced

2 tablespoons chopped garlic

½ pint grape or Sungold
tomatoes, halved

1¼ pounds fresh shell beans
(about 2 cups shelled)

½ pound collard greens,
stems discarded and
roughly chopped

2 cups fresh corn kernels
(about 3 ears)

2 tablespoons chopped
fresh savory

Kosher salt, to taste

Black pepper, to taste

Prepare chicken. In a bowl, mix together all ingredients except chicken. Coat chicken in mixture and marinate for 8 to 10 hours.

Preheat grill to high. Drain marinated chicken and grill 3 minutes on each side. Lower heat to medium and finish cooking chicken, about 20 minutes, rotating so as to not burn the outside.

Prepare the beans. In a medium pot, heat olive oil over medium-high heat. Add bacon, cook until well browned (about 5 to 6 minutes), remove from pot, and set aside. Add onions and cook until just past golden brown, about 12 to 15 minutes, stirring frequently. Add garlic and cook for 3 minutes. Add tomatoes and cook for 8 to 10 minutes.

Add beans and 5 cups water. Bring to a boil then reduce heat and simmer for 15 minutes. Add collard greens and simmer for another 10 minutes. Add corn, savory, bacon, and a pinch of salt and pepper. Simmer for 2 minutes more. Remove from heat and season to taste with salt and pepper.

Spoon the beans onto plates. Place chicken on top and garnish with a heaping spoonful of Grilled Okra and Green Tomato Relish (pg. 121). Serve with cornbread.

GRILLED OKRA *and* GREEN TOMATO RELISH

MAKES 2 CUPS

¼ pound okra

2 green tomatoes
(about ¾ pound), sliced

1 small red onion, sliced

3 tablespoons olive oil, divided

Kosher salt, to taste

Black pepper, to taste

2 tablespoons Beer Mustard
(pg. 231)

2 tablespoons cider vinegar

1 tablespoon honey

2 tablespoons chopped parsley

Preheat grill to high. Keeping the vegetables separate, lightly coat okra, tomatoes, and onions with olive oil and season with a pinch of salt and pepper. Grill okra until they start to blister, about 10 to 12 minutes. Grill tomatoes for about 3 to 4 minutes on each side, and grill onion slices for about 8 to 10 minutes on each side. Remove vegetables from grill and let cool.

In a bowl, mix together the Beer Mustard, cider vinegar, honey, and parsley. Chop the grilled vegetables and combine with vinegar mixture. Season to taste with salt and pepper.

Produce Spotlight

OKRA

IN recent years, few vegetables have revealed our customers' changing tastes like okra. Al planted okra decades ago, but it languished in the stand and he deemed the unloved plant a horrible failure. Recently, however, customer requests have poured in, so we decided to try it once more. We plant just a few rows, but so far it is enough to satisfy demand.

The heat-loving plant starts slow then majestically rises in the field. Its beautiful, creamy white blooms open under an umbrella of leaves. As the flower fades, the edible seedpod takes shape. While okra may not be a New England farmstand staple yet, our customers love it and we continue to appease its cult following.

VEGETABLE FRIED CAULIFLOWER RICE

SERVES 4 TO 6

3 tablespoons sesame oil, divided

2 teaspoons chopped garlic

3 teaspoons chopped ginger

1 head cauliflower, grated into rice-size pieces (about 4 to 6 cups)

¼ head broccoli, grated into rice-size pieces (about 1 cup)

1 cup chopped scallions

1 medium carrot, shredded

½ cup fresh peas

½ bell pepper, chopped

2 eggs, beaten

3 tablespoons soy sauce

2 heads baby bok choy, thinly sliced

Kosher salt, to taste

2 tablespoons black sesame seeds, for garnish

Heat 2 tablespoons sesame oil in a large sauté pan or wok over medium-high heat. Add garlic and ginger and cook for 30 seconds. Add cauliflower and brown for 1 minute without stirring. Add broccoli, scallions, carrots, peas, and bell pepper. Cook for 1 minute, stirring a few times. Add eggs and cook for 1 minute, stirring to cook the eggs evenly. Add soy sauce and cook for 30 seconds. Remove from heat and set aside.

Cook the bok choy. Heat remaining tablespoon sesame oil in a large sauté pan or wok over medium-high heat. Add bok choy and pinch of salt. Stir and cook for 30 seconds, remove from pan.

Divide the cauliflower rice onto plates then top with bok choy and black sesame seeds. We love this dish with sliced Char Sui Pork (pg. 125) on top.

⊢ *Produce Spotlight* ⊢

CAULIFLOWER

A staple of crudité platters for decades, this unassuming vegetable requires more real estate in the field per plant than any other. Cauliflower plants grow almost three feet in each direction. Large, bluish-green leaves branch out to catch late-summer sun and concentrate on forming the head deep in the center. After months of tending to the crop and protecting it from caterpillars, birds, and deer, we are rewarded with one perfect bundle of curds per plant. We tie the leaves together above the heads to block the sun and blanch them to a blazing white. Some varieties will produce heads of a different color. The bright orange of Cheddar, the psychedelic purple of Graffiti, and even the spiky green of romanesco each add a touch of flair to an otherwise pale veggie platter.

CHAR SUI PORK

SERVES 4 TO 6

ROASTED BEET PURÉE

1 medium beet, rinsed and greens discarded

1 tablespoon olive oil

Pinch of kosher salt

¼ cup rice vinegar

CHAR SUI PORK

½ cup hoisin sauce

½ cup Roasted Beet Purée

3 tablespoons honey

2 tablespoons sesame oil

3 teaspoons chopped ginger

2 teaspoons chopped garlic

1 teaspoon soy sauce

¾ teaspoon Chinese five-spice powder

2 pounds pork tenderloin

Preheat oven to 400°F.

Make purée. Lightly coat beet with olive oil and a pinch of salt. Roast in a baking dish until tender, about 45 to 60 minutes. Remove from oven and let cool. Using a paper towel, wipe the skin off of the beet, purée beet in a blender or food processor, then scoop into a mixing bowl. Mix in vinegar and store in refrigerator for up to 5 days.

Make pork. In a bowl, combine all ingredients except pork. Once sauce is mixed, set aside ¼ cup. Coat pork with remaining sauce, cover, and refrigerate for 24 hours.

Remove pork from marinade; preheat half of grill to high and the other to medium-low.

Grill pork over high heat until all sides achieve grill marks, about 10 minutes. Move pork over to medium-low heat and grill to desired doneness. Let sit for 8 minutes before slicing.

Spoon Roasted Beet Purée over pork slices and serve with Vegetable Fried Cauliflower Rice (pg. 122).

INDIAN SPICED CHICKEN *with* TOMATO CHUTNEY

CHICKEN

½ cup chopped scallions

3 cloves garlic

2 tablespoons chopped ginger

2 teaspoons Garam Masala
(pg. 227)

2 cups plain yogurt

1 tablespoon lime juice

4 to 6 boneless, skinless
chicken breasts, halved

Kosher salt, to taste

TOMATO CHUTNEY

2½ pounds assorted tomatoes

1 teaspoon olive oil

1½ teaspoons whole
cumin seed

1½ teaspoons whole
mustard seed

2 tablespoons chopped garlic

2 tablespoons chopped ginger

⅓ cup plus 2 tablespoons
cider vinegar

Kosher salt, to taste

2½ tablespoons
granulated sugar

2 tablespoons
chopped cilantro

Prepare the chicken. Place scallions, garlic, ginger, and Garam Masala in a food processor. Run for 30 seconds. Add yogurt and lime juice and run another 30 seconds. Set marinade aside.

Place chicken into a bowl and coat with marinade. Cover and refrigerate for at least 4 hours or overnight.

Preheat oven to 350°F.

Line a sheet pan with foil. Remove chicken from marinade and discard excess. Arrange chicken pieces on sheet pan and sprinkle each with salt. Bake about 20 to 25 minutes or until internal temperature reaches 155°F to 160°F.

Make chutney. Core, deseed, and dice the tomatoes. Heat olive oil in a saucepan over medium heat. Add cumin and mustard seeds and cook until fragrant, about 10 seconds. Add garlic and ginger and cook for 30 seconds. Add vinegar, a pinch of salt, and tomatoes. Simmer for 20 minutes, stirring frequently.

Add sugar and simmer another 10 minutes. Remove from heat and let cool. Add cilantro. Adjust seasoning if necessary, and refrigerate in a sealed container until needed.

Remove chicken from oven, plate, and spoon 2 tablespoons of Tomato Chutney on top of each piece. Be sure to keep a bowl of chutney on the table in case people want more. (They will.)

This chutney will keep in the refrigerator for up to 5 days and in the freezer for up to 6 months.

PEACH POLENTA UPSIDE-DOWN CAKE

MAKES ONE 9-INCH CAKE ─────────────────────────────

FILLING

2 tablespoons salted butter

⅓ cup brown sugar

2 cups ripe peaches, sliced about ¼-inch thick

1 teaspoon lemon juice (optional)

CAKE

¾ cup whole milk

1 tablespoon vanilla extract

1 cup fresh corn kernels (about 1 to 2 ears)

1 cup all-purpose flour

½ cup polenta or fine cornmeal

1 tablespoon chopped thyme (optional)

1 teaspoon baking powder

½ teaspoon iodized salt

1½ sticks unsalted butter, at room temperature

1 cup granulated sugar

3 eggs

3 egg yolks

Preheat oven to 325°F.

Make filling. Melt butter with brown sugar in a 9-inch cast iron skillet over medium-low heat. Stir until bubbling, then remove from heat and set aside.

Toss peaches with lemon juice (if using). Set aside.

Make cake batter. In a bowl, mix together milk, vanilla extract, and corn kernels and set aside. In a separate bowl, mix together flour, polenta, thyme (if using), baking powder, and salt and set aside.

Using a hand mixer or stand mixer fitted with the paddle attachment, cream butter and sugar on high until very light and fluffy, about 3 to 5 minutes. Reduce speed to medium, slowly add eggs and yolks, and mix for 2 minutes. Scrape down sides of bowl and mix for an additional minute. The mixture may look curdled but it is fine.

Reduce speed to low. Slowly add some of flour mixture, followed by milk mixture. Continue until both mixtures are fully incorporated into a thick batter.

Fan peach slices on top of brown sugar mixture in skillet. Spoon batter over peaches, taking care not to disturb the fan design.

Bake until golden brown and cake springs back slightly in center, about 40 to 50 minutes. Remove from oven and let cool for 20 minutes. Run knife around edge of pan. With oven mitts, carefully invert onto serving platter. Serve peach side up, slightly warm or at room temperature.

CHOCOLATE ZUCCHINI CAKE

3 cups grated zucchini

2⅔ cups granulated sugar, divided

4 eggs

1 cup vegetable oil

2 cups all-purpose flour

¾ cup unsweetened cocoa powder

2 teaspoons baking soda

1 teaspoon baking powder

½ teaspoon iodized salt

1 teaspoon ground cinnamon

¾ cup chocolate chips

Powdered sugar, for dusting

Preheat oven to 325°F.

Grease a 9-inch cake pan with butter or cooking spray. Line pan with a circle of parchment paper, then grease again.

Toss grated zucchini with 1 cup sugar then let strain for 5 to 10 minutes. Press to squeeze out any excess liquid. Transfer zucchini to a bowl and, using a spatula, stir in eggs and oil.

In a separate bowl, stir together the flour, remaining sugar, cocoa powder, baking soda, baking powder, salt, cinnamon, and chocolate chips. Fold this dry mixture into the zucchini mixture with a spatula, mixing to fully incorporate. Spread batter evenly into prepared pan.

Bake until a toothpick inserted in the center comes out clean, about 50 to 60 minutes. Remove from oven and let cool for 40 minutes before unmolding.

Top with powdered sugar and serve at room temperature.

LAVENDER SUGAR COOKIES

1 tablespoon dried lavender flowers

⅔ cup granulated sugar, plus more for dusting

2 teaspoons finely grated lemon zest

2 sticks unsalted butter

1½ teaspoons vanilla extract

2 cups all-purpose flour

Pinch of iodized salt

Place lavender flowers, ⅔ cup sugar, and lemon zest in a food processor. Pulse 10 to 15 times until well combined.

Using a hand mixer or stand mixer fitted with the paddle attachment, cream butter and sugar on high until very light and fluffy, about 3 to 5 minutes. Reduce speed to medium, add vanilla extract, and mix for another 2 minutes, scraping down bowl halfway through. Add flour and salt and mix on low for 2 minutes, scraping down bowl halfway through.

Dump mixture onto a lightly floured countertop or cutting board. Form dough into a 12-inch log. Wrap log in plastic and refrigerate for at least 1 hour or overnight.

Liberally grease a baking sheet and preheat oven to 325°F.

Remove log from refrigerator and cut into ½-inch-thick slices. Dip both sides of each slice in granulated sugar and place on greased baking sheet about 1 inch apart.

Bake until very lightly golden, about 17 minutes. Remove from oven and let cool for 5 minutes before transferring from baking sheet.

These cookies will keep in a sealed container at room temperature for 5 days.

BELLINI

Tim Grejtak

The Bellini is a sophisticated Italian cocktail invented in 1945 by Giuseppe Cipriani at Harry's Bar in Venice. It was named for the fifteenth-century Italian artist Jacopo Bellini, whose works had a pink glow, just like the cocktail. We served a version of this classic cocktail at our first Dinner in the Field but have come to love it with the addition of a little grapefruit liqueur as well.

MAKES 1 DRINK

1 white peach

2 to 3 ice cubes

½ teaspoon fresh lemon juice

½ ounce Pamplemousse Grapefruit Liqueur (optional)

3½ ounces chilled prosecco

In a blender, purée the peach, including the skin, with ice cubes and lemon juice.

Pour 2 ounces of the peach purée and optional grapefruit liqueur into a champagne flute. Slowly add the chilled prosecco, stirring constantly to incorporate.

Al watering tomatoes in the greenhouse, 1970s.

VOLANTE FARMS
— Fall —
AL & MEL

Left: Al and Mel on their wedding day, 1976; right: Mel pricing watermelons in the farmstand, early 1980s.

NEEDHAM 1973

By the spring of 1973, Ferdinand was feeling the fatigue of decades of farming. Not only had key members of the family started to retire, some of the laborers who had followed them from the Newton farm had grown ill, old, or were otherwise ready to move on. When Anne retired, her steady hand with the farm's finances was missed. Three important managers who had started with the family at the Newton farm—the field manager, the produce manager, the farmstand manager—also left that year. This sudden transition was almost the end of the family's long farming history.

Al had plans to study plant and soil sciences at the University of Massachusetts in Amherst, but Ferdinand told him that the farm likely wouldn't be there when he came back. Faced with this news, Al quickly enrolled at Babson College, which was just around the corner. Though not his initial plan, it proved to be the perfect step toward launching his tenure at the farm. Al's sister Helen graduated from the University of Massachusetts in Amherst the previous

year and took a full-time job as a nutritionist away from the farm. Al was tossed the reins of a challenging business.

That summer, the Town of Needham began a large reconstruction project on Central Avenue. The pavement from Owen's Poultry Farm to Great Plain Avenue was torn up, drastically reducing traffic by the farm for that whole season. Al saw this roadwork as a blessing in disguise. He took advantage of the slow months by cutting crop sizes and reducing the output of the entire operation while he got a handle on his schooling and managing the farm.

By 1974, the town had repaired the road and the pace of traffic by the farm increased. Al was working hard on an accelerated course of study at Babson so he could turn his attention back to the farm, where Helen was now working part time. He began updating the farm's business practices and officially incorporated the farm with his sister. In December of 1975, Al graduated from Babson with a degree in business management.

Feeling the pressures of running a family business, he soon learned that long motorcycle rides helped to clear his head. In April of 1974, feeling overworked and suffering from a bout of mononucleosis, he went tooling around on his Honda CB750. That is when he met Melodie (Mel) Hahn, who was waiting tables at a restaurant in Dedham. Soon after, Mel started working at the farm on weekends and during her days off from her full-time job at Sears.

Mel started on the register but was soon tackling any job she could get her hands on. With her electric attitude, she quickly won the approval of the family. Ferdinand was particularly impressed that she knew how to properly use a push broom, of all things. She knew that marrying Al meant marrying into the family business, so in 1976 she quit her job at Sears to work full-time at the farm. She found her calling getting her hands dirty in the greenhouse, and in doing so she developed a close bond with Ferdinand. On October 16, 1976, Al and Mel married at St. Bartholomew's Parish in Needham and started their life together. Meanwhile in 1975, having recently returned to the farm full-time, Helen met and fell for one of the field workers, Peter MacArthur. Helen and Peter married in the fall of 1976, right before Al and Mel.

The four newlyweds ran the farm together as partners for more than three years. They lived together in Helen and Al's childhood home, which had been converted into a two-family house. This setup allowed the young Volante siblings to decide on the true direction of the farm's future. Ferdinand had some very strong opinions, which he voiced on a regular basis, but ultimately it was up to his children to make their own decisions. After the 1979 season, Helen and Peter left the family farm to strike out on their own. Pursuing an opportunity to build on a plot of land along Route 126 in Holliston, they built a greenhouse and stand and launched MacArthur Farm the following year. Today their farm continues to produce for several greater Boston farmers markets.

Al and Mel then went to work to update and modernize the farm. They removed old sash houses, tore out cold frames and steam pipes, and replaced the leveled buildings with more modern structures, such as wide, plastic-covered hoop houses. These new structures were more efficient and had better conditions for growing and retail sales.

Clockwise from top left: Ferdinand on Al's motorcycle, 1970; Mel and Al at her bridal shower, 1976; Peter MacArthur with Helen, watering the geraniums, 1970s; the farm truck parked in the field, 1970s.

GREENWAYS

Around the time Al and Mel were making improvements, Helen Greenway approached Al about farming some of her beautiful acreage along Charles River Street. In many ways, Helen Greenway was ahead of her time. She saw the benefit of eating locally grown food and loved the idea of putting her fallow land back into production. She partnered with the Volantes to make her dream a reality. Nestled amid hundred-foot white pines, the fields push up against long-standing apple orchards, woods, and abandoned railroad paths leading down to the Charles River. The fields have views of a fish pond, old brick sheds, and hollows left by the foundations of grand (but forgotten) structures.

The leased land covered part of the old Baker Estate's Ridge Hill Farms, which hold a unique spot in Needham's history. The Baker Estate was a popular amusement park in the late 1800s. Guests traveled in droves to visit it and stay at the Hotel Wellesley, one of the area's most luxurious hotels. William Emerson Baker was an eccentric millionaire. In addition to his lavish parties and fanciful animal exhibits, he sought to change the way people interacted with their food and its sources. To help accomplish this, he created the amusement park and resort to highlight his vision of clean eating and living. His estate became a beacon for modern agricultural experimentation. Though most of the buildings—including the Sanitary Piggery—are gone today, the Volantes were able to revive the land and reinstate part of both Baker's and Mrs. Greenway's agricultural visions.

Al plowed the Greenways' land for the first time in October of 1976. With the ongoing support and generosity of the Greenways, the Volante family still farms these fields to this day. The Greenways' land is high, dry, and easy to work compared to most other Needham farmland.

THE NEW FARMSTAND

The day after Columbus Day in 1981, demolition began on the old farmstand. Al moved retail sales to one of the newer greenhouses for the remainder of October. Vinny Youdis, the family's neighbor, rolled his excavator down Brookside Road to demolish the old building while Al began removing its roof. Ferdinand stood below him, shouting, "Do you know how many taxes you'll have to pay?!" In spite of this warning, Al and his crew completed the new building on schedule and opened for the Christmas season that year.

The new farmstand was clean, airy, well lit, and inviting. There were several garage doors that opened to welcome in customers. Additionally, a set of doors leading into the back room was installed so that the crew no longer had to crawl under the counter to get inside. Eventually there was even an office with air conditioning, heat, and a wood stove that was perfect for drying wet winter gloves. It was truly 20th century living. While the farmstand was undergoing upgrades, Mel and Al built a new home for their growing family on the site of the old Woodcock farmhouse. They now had a lovely view overlooking their fields.

Sales went through the new roof, prompting Al to find more land and laborers. The enhanced retail experience on the farm had Al considering heating the entire stand with hot air from the greenhouse. Mel and manager Molly Lyne implored him not to do it,

Left: An inside view of the farmstand, 2000; right: geraniums and hangers lined the walkway in front of the new farmstand.

Clockwise from left: Al on the new John Deere tractor, 1980; our Standish field in 1991; a bird's eye view of the main farm, with the newly built farmstand, early 1980s.

fearing that a heated farmstand would encourage Al to stay open year-round. Al still thinks listening to them was the best decision he ever made.

Just as the Volantes had discovered decades before, others began to see Needham as an attractive alternative to Newton. As the population and the farm's customer base grew, Al and Mel sought more fields to increase their yields. Their search led them to Needham's Standish Road.

STANDISH

Al bought the Standish Road fields in 1991 from Winslow's Nursery. These fifty-five acres are surrounded by man-made ponds fed by Fuller Brook and are overlooked by the Needham radio towers and Ridge Hill Reservation. It took a couple of years to turn the overgrown and pockmarked nursery into a vegetable farm. Huge holes dotted the landscape where large trees had been removed. To this day, there are many unique, non-native species of trees growing

there—tall larches, enormous white birches, thick beeches, willows, and the random evergreen or magnolia among them. Clearing the overgrown shrubs and trees was a huge undertaking, but Ungie took it up fervently as it meant ample opportunity for him to forage for mushrooms in the woods—when he wasn't burning piles of brush and chasing away groundhogs and geese. In those first years, crops that required less cultivation, like pumpkins and winter squash, filled the rows in between crabapple trees.

Today, Standish Farm is a peaceful refuge. Its soil is classified as Sudbury soil, which is considered prime farmland. The smooth fields have few rocks. Red-tailed hawks and other raptors soar overhead, fussing with the crows and hunting a bit in the fields.

The Greenway and Standish fields produce the bulk of the corn, tomatoes, and other large format crops. About half of the land at Standish is designated the Anne Volante Conservation Area in honor of Ferdinand's wife and Al's mother, who passed away

in 1988. With the Ridge Hill Reservation and other attached properties, it makes up one of the largest tracts of undeveloped land in the town.

In the early days, Standish became the go-to location for employee farm picnics, specifically the annual Clam Jam that celebrates the peak of harvest season. The entire Volante family and their crew gathered among the crops, picking fresh corn to boil on the spot, grilling burgers, and enjoying steamers with a side of volleyball, badminton, or softball. The family and staff still meet and barbecue at the Clam Jam each year. To Al's dismay, lobsters have replaced clams.

ORCHARD PARTNERSHIPS

Much like his father, Al cultivated relationships with other farmers in the area. In addition to farmers within the vegetable and berry communities, he reached out to New England's tree fruit growers. Customers were itching for apples and stone fruit, but the two Seckel pear trees and Ungie's few peach trees would only yield enough fruit for the family. Al turned to growers like Chip Hardy of Brookdale Fruit Farm in Hollis, New Hampshire and Bill Broderick of Sunny Crest Orchards in Sterling, Massachusetts. Volante Farms could now add fresh, fuzzy peaches, golden nectarines, Italian prune plums, and up to eighty varieties of apples to its growing list of offerings at the stand.

With help from these local partners, Al turned apple season into one of the farm's biggest annual attractions. In the fall, tents popped up to house the wooden apple bins overflowing with varieties ranging from century-old heirlooms to sweet snacking apples.

As apple season faded and thousands of hardy mums brought color to browning gardens, the farm rolled into Halloween season. Truckload after truckload of pumpkins arrived from growers in Concord, Ipswich, and the Pioneer Valley. The crew hurled pumpkins between one another from the flatbeds to the benches for display. During those years, the crop selection waned after the late-October frost came through. Corn would be lucky to last until Columbus Day, and any leftover stalks became fall decor. The frost and then Halloween would mark the end of the growing season for Al, Mel, and the crew. Come November, they would sweep, scrub, and shutter the stand. They would then enjoy a brief respite before Thanksgiving and the arrival of the Christmas tree trucks.

FARMERS IN RETIREMENT

Ferdinand and Ungie continued working at the farm with Al and Mel right through the 1990s. Ferdinand, unburdened from the day-to-day task of running of the farm, would arrive before dawn to wash and set up the lettuce display and sort tomatoes for ripeness, often singing from his Italian songbook. He took time on his way out the door to yell at the field crew for being so slow with the morning's harvest—even though it was only seven o'clock.

Ungie was a little less involved in daily farm activities, but he was never absent for long. He kept up his fig and peach trees and tended to his Concord grape trellises. At one point, nearly every greenhouse on the farm had one of his figs growing in it. He would prune and wrap them for the winter and sneak them some fertilizer with a little help from field manager Lee. It wasn't until the new stand was built in 2012 that the last of his fig trees was uprooted from the greenhouse—although it still lives on in a large pot.

While Ferdinand took great pleasure in challenging his son's decisions and methods, he also loved spending time with his family and the farm crew. He had a knack for knowing when people needed a special thanks or morale boost. Sometimes it would come in the form of his exquisitely roasted cornetta peppers, delivered on a cool fall morning, oily and warm on a foil-lined cookie sheet with a loaf of crunchy Cavagni's bread (recipe pg. 182). Other times it was a plastic shopping bag—full but light as a feather—landing on a register table during the frigid Christmas season. Inside the bag would be freshly popped corn flavored with a touch of olive oil and plenty of salt.

Come January, Ferdinand and Ungie enjoyed the quiet of the farm. They would meet in the greenhouse at dawn to seed the crops for the coming spring's bedding plants. They used a modern machine to do this, directing the tiny seeds to their new homes, but their aging eyes and unsteady aim often left the greenhouse floor carpeted in seeds. By mid-March, a jungle would be growing underfoot. The two brothers spent their lives working together, forming a bond forged of sweat and dirt. They were side by side until the very end, each passing away in the summer of 2002, only thirteen days apart.

Ferdinand and Ungie weren't the only members of their generation to carry their weight on the farm. Mel's father Jack Hahn helped with bookkeeping for twenty years after retiring from music education. Joining the farm to work alongside his family fulfilled him. He often remarked how hard the life of a farmer was and how proud he was of his family for doing it. He wore his Volante Farms jacket with pride, prompting some long-winded conversations with passersby. Later in life, he visited the farm often and always brought a smile to employees' faces. He passed away in 2015, and his ever-positive attitude and charming demeanor is greatly missed.

Clockwise from top left: Brothers Ferdinand, Ungie, and Peter, with a young Steve, 1990s; Anne and Ferdinand on their backyard bocce court, 1980s; Jack "Papa ZZ" Hahn and his pooch, Phantom, 1990s; Ferdinand's best friend, Elio Angelucci, 1990s.

FALL

COOLER NIGHTS USHER in a hectic fall harvest, as all the season's crops are eager to complete their production cycle. In September, which is often the busiest month on the farm, everything growing in the fields is ready to come out of the ground and off the vine. Brassicas and winter squash join the fresh offerings in the farmstand. It is awash in apples, with up to eighty varieties over the course of the season and up to thirty available on any given day. Bushels of storage crops, like carrots and parsnips, are pulled from the ground to keep our coffers full through the slower, colder months. The first damaging frost usually falls around Columbus Day, and by Thanksgiving, the last of the cold hardy vegetables are harvested from the field.

Fall Recipes

LATE HARVEST BROCCOLI *and* CHEDDAR SOUP

2 heads broccoli (about 2 pounds)

2 tablespoons salted butter

1 medium yellow onion, chopped

2 tablespoons chopped garlic

1½ quarts chicken stock

Kosher salt, to taste

Black pepper, to taste

4 ounces baby spinach

½ cup light cream

1 cup grated cheddar cheese

Separate the broccoli florets from the stems and roughly chop. Discard the tough bottom ends of the stem and thinly slice the rest.

Melt butter in a large pot over medium-high heat. Add onions and cook until golden brown, about 10 to 12 minutes. Add garlic and cook for 2 minutes. Add stock and increase heat to high. Bring to a boil. Lower heat to medium and simmer for 10 minutes.

Add broccoli stems and cook until almost tender, about 6 to 8 minutes. Add florets and a pinch of salt and pepper and cook until tender, about 4 minutes. Remove from heat.

Stir in spinach and let it wilt, about 2 minutes. Add cream. Purée soup in the pot with an immersion blender. If you don't have an immersion blender, purée in small batches in a traditional blender and return the soup to the pot.

Fold in cheese and season to taste with salt and pepper. Serve hot with a side of crusty bread.

CORN

CORN is the quintessential farmstand vegetable. From the 1960s through the 1980s, corn was king at Volante Farms. No other product on the farm—except for perhaps Christmas trees—is tracked with such precision. We now dedicate nearly half of our thirty acres to corn in a given season, which begins in mid-July and runs through Columbus Day. Corn takes about eighty days to ripen and has a short harvest window. Therefore, we need to know three months in advance how much corn to plant each week in order to have enough available in the farmstand on any given summer day. Our corn records go back to the 1960s and include bushels sold, weather, holidays, general temperament, road closures—anything that could impact sales on a day-to-day basis. In 2015, we made the monumental jump from paper to a computer spreadsheet. At first, it was a disturbing change in protocol, but we quickly found that portable data was an asset on such a busy farm.

Corn is at its best the day it is picked. While modern varieties hold their sugar well, there is still nothing like freshly picked corn. In fact, the field crew prefers to sample raw ears right in the field, a critical quality-control check. They head out at seven o'clock in the morning, dressed head-to-toe in rain suits and water boots, with a sack full of sacks. Their steamy outfits keep them somewhat dry from the dew and protect them from the sharp edges of the corn leaves as they tear down the rows. Each cornstalk, which can range in height from five to seven feet, provides us with one marketable ear of corn. Each pair of pickers rips corn off the stalk with a quick flick and twist of the wrist. Armloads of ten ears are dropped into a bagger's sack. After filling each bushel bag, the bounty is lugged to the nearest sack row for pickup. The corn truck returns to the stand and we pour the first fresh bags of corn onto the table by the time the doors open at eight o'clock.

If you have to store your corn, preserve its freshness by keeping it cool in your refrigerator with the husk on. Our "please don't tear me apart" plea that hangs over the corn table is for the benefit of the corn. Once the husk is peeled back, the quality immediately begins to fade. We sort through the table several times a day and are glad to hand over our favorite ears; a practiced hand can tell a plump, juicy ear right through the husk. In fact, one of Al's first jobs on the farm was to stand at the corn table and hand customers the number of ears they wanted. It was a big shift in policy to allow customers to choose their own ears.

The simplest method for preparing our corn is to boil a big pot of water, shuck the corn, and toss it in for three minutes at the most. Butter and salt the steaming ears as desired, though it's so good, we find this unnecessary.

SOUTHWESTERN CORN *and* BACON CHOWDER

1 pound Yukon Gold potatoes

4 cups Corn Stock (pg. 157) or chicken stock

Kosher salt, to taste

3 tablespoons salted butter, divided

⅓ cup diced bacon (about 2 slices)

1 large yellow onion, chopped

1½ tablespoons chopped garlic

½ teaspoon ground cumin

¾ teaspoon dried oregano

¼ teaspoon ground coriander, toasted

1½ teaspoons chipotle purée, store bought

Black pepper, to taste

½ cup light cream

1 red bell pepper, small diced

6 cups fresh corn kernels (about 8 ears), divided

1 tablespoon chopped cilantro

Dice the potatoes into ½-inch pieces and set half aside. Add the stock, a pinch of salt, and half of the potatoes to a pot and bring to a boil. Immediately reduce heat and simmer until potatoes are just cooked through but still firm, about 15 minutes. Remove potatoes, rinse under cold water, set aside, and reserve stock.

Melt 1 tablespoon butter in a large pot over medium-high heat. Add bacon and cook until golden brown, about 8 minutes. Remove bacon and set aside. Add onions and cook until golden brown, 8 to 10 minutes. Add garlic and cook for 3 minutes. Add cumin, oregano, and coriander and cook for 1 minute.

Add uncooked potatoes, half of the corn, chipotle purée, and reserved stock to the pot and season with a pinch of salt and pepper. Bring to a boil, then reduce to a simmer, cooking until the potatoes start to break apart, about 18 to 20 minutes.

Stir in light cream and purée soup with an immersion blender. If you don't have an immersion blender, purée in small batches in a traditional blender and return the soup to the pot.

Add remaining butter to a large sauté pan over medium-high heat. Add the diced bell pepper and cook for 8 minutes. Add corn and cook for 1 minute more, then add to the soup along with the cooked diced potatoes, bacon, and cilantro.

Season to taste with salt and pepper and serve warm.

CORN STOCK

8 corn cobs

1 small yellow onion, chopped

1 small carrot, peeled and chopped

2 stalks celery

2 cloves garlic

Few sprigs of thyme and parsley

1 fresh bay leaf

Place everything into a pot with 3 quarts water. Bring to a boil then reduce to a simmer.

Simmer for 1½ hours, drain, and discard vegetables. Use as a base for Southwestern Corn and Bacon Chowder (pg. 154), Summer Vegetable Pasta (pg. 104), or in any soup that might benefit from a summery corn flavor.

TOMATO *and* CORN TART

CRUST

7 tablespoons salted butter, cubed, cold

1½ cups all-purpose flour

¼ cup fine cornmeal

⅓ cup grated Parmesan cheese

½ teaspoon black pepper

2 tablespoons olive oil

3 tablespoons cold water

FILLING

2 tablespoons olive oil

1 small yellow onion, diced

1 tablespoon chopped garlic

1½ cups fresh corn kernels (about 2 ears)

1 tablespoon chopped marjoram

Kosher salt, to taste

Black pepper, to taste

⅔ cup grated Fontina cheese

¾ pound heirloom tomatoes, thinly sliced

1 large egg, beaten

Freeze cubed butter for 10 minutes prior to making crust.

Make crust. In a food processor, mix together flour, cornmeal, Parmesan cheese, and black pepper. Pulse for 10 seconds, and then add chilled butter, olive oil, and water. Pulse until dough starts to come together, about 30 seconds.

Place dough onto a floured work surface and knead into a ball. Add a little cold water if too dry and crumbly. Flatten dough into a disk, wrap in plastic, and let rest at room temperature for 1 hour.

Make the filling. Heat olive oil in a large sauté pan over medium-high heat. Add onions and cook until golden brown, about 8 to 10 minutes. Add garlic and cook for 1 minute. Add corn kernels and cook for 1 minute. Remove from heat and add marjoram and a pinch of salt and pepper. Allow to cool completely and then mix in Fontina.

Preheat oven to 400°F.

Lightly flour both sides of the dough and roll it out into a large circle, about 12 inches in diameter with ¼-inch thickness. Place dough on a sheet pan and spread corn mixture on top, leaving a 2-inch border.

Pat dry the tomato slices and arrange on top of corn. Fold dough border over corn and tomatoes. Sprinkle with salt and pepper and lightly brush dough with egg. Bake until golden brown, about 30 to 35 minutes.

Remove from oven and serve warm.

CORN, OKRA, *and* BACON FRITTERS

SERVES 4 TO 6

¼ **pound okra**

3 **tablespoons canola or grapeseed oil, divided, plus more for frying**

⅓ **cup diced bacon (about 2 slices)**

1 **large egg**

¾ **cup buttermilk**

1 **cup fresh corn kernels (about 1 to 2 ears)**

1 **scallion, chopped**

½ **tablespoon kosher salt, plus more to taste**

Pinch of cayenne pepper

Black pepper, to taste

1 **cup fine cornmeal**

1½ **tablespoons all-purpose flour**

⅛ **teaspoon baking soda**

Remove and discard okra stems. Split lengthwise and remove seeds. Chop okra to the size of corn kernels.

Heat 1 tablespoon oil in a large sauté pan over medium-high heat. Add bacon and cook until golden brown, about 5 to 6 minutes. Remove from pan and cool.

In a large bowl, whisk together egg and buttermilk. Add corn, bacon, okra, scallion, 1/2 tablespoon of salt, a pinch of black pepper, and a pinch of cayenne pepper. In a separate bowl, mix together the cornmeal, flour, and baking soda. Add to the wet ingredients and mix to combine.

Heat 2 tablespoons oil in a large, nonstick pan over medium-high heat. Scoop fritter mixture, 2 tablespoons at a time, into pan, leaving room between the fritters so as not to crowd the pan. Cook until golden brown, about 2 to 3 minutes, flip, and cook another 2 minutes. Remove from pan and keep warm. Repeat with remaining batter, adding more oil if pan becomes dry. Serve warm topped with Spicy Tomato Jam.

SPICY TOMATO JAM

This is a versatile condiment. You can serve it with pork or chicken or simply spread it on a sand-wich. If you omit the jalapeño, it pairs well with goat cheese or pecorino on a piece of crusty bread.

MAKES 1 PINT

¼ teaspoon whole cumin seed

1 tablespoon olive oil

1 shallot, diced

1 jalapeño, deseeded
and diced

1 tablespoon chopped garlic

2 pints grape or
Sungold tomatoes

Kosher salt, to taste

Black pepper, to taste

1 tablespoon cider vinegar

⅓ cup granulated sugar

Toast cumin seeds in a dry pan over medium heat until fragrant and browned, about 1 to 2 minutes. Add olive oil to pot and cook for 30 seconds. Add shallot and cook for 2 minutes. Add jalapeño and garlic and cook for 1 minute. Increase heat to medium-high and add toma-toes and a pinch of salt and pepper.

Cook until tomatoes start to burst, about 5 minutes. Add vinegar and cook for 1 minute, smashing the tomatoes. Add sugar, stirring often, and bring to a boil. Then lower heat and simmer until mixture thickens, about 20 minutes. Remove from heat and season to taste with salt and pepper.

This jam will keep in the refrigerator for 12 days.

WHEATBERRY SALAD *with* BEETS, KALE, *and* SMOKED APPLE VINAIGRETTE

SERVES 4

2 to 3 beets (about 1 pound), tops removed

2 tablespoons olive oil

1½ cups wheatberries, soaked in water overnight

Kosher salt, to taste

Black pepper, to taste

1 bunch kale, stems discarded and finely chopped

1 cup Smoked Apple Vinaigrette

⅓ cup blue cheese, crumbled, divided

⅓ cup chopped Marcona almonds, divided

Preheat oven to 400°F.

Rinse beets well, drizzle with olive oil, and wrap tightly in foil. Bake until tender, about 45 minutes to 1 hour. Let cool in foil for 15 minutes, remove skins with a paper towel, cut beets into quarters, and set aside.

Drain the wheatberries and add to a pot with 3 cups of water and a pinch of salt and pepper. Bring to a boil, then lower heat and simmer until tender, about 40 to 50 minutes. Strain wheatberries, immediately toss with kale, and let cool for 15 minutes.

In a large bowl, mix together wheatberries, beets, Smoked Apple Vinaigrette, and half of the blue cheese and Marcona almonds.

Divide onto plates and garnish with the remaining cheese and almonds.

SMOKED APPLE VINAIGRETTE

MAKES ABOUT 1 PINT

2 Honeycrisp apples

1¼ cups extra virgin olive oil, divided

1 tablespoon chopped sage

1 tablespoon honey

1 teaspoon smoked paprika

Kosher salt, to taste

Black pepper, to taste

¼ cup cider vinegar

2 tablespoons apple cider

1 tablespoon whole grain mustard

Preheat oven to 350°F.

Peel, core, and chop the apples. Toss apples with ¼ cup olive oil, sage, honey, paprika, and a pinch of salt and pepper. Place on a foil-lined sheet pan and roast for 20 minutes. Remove and let cool.

Place roasted apples, cider vinegar, apple cider, and mustard in a blender. Pulse for 30 seconds, then scrape down the sides and pulse for another 10 seconds. With the blender still running, slowly pour in remaining olive oil. Season to taste with salt and pepper.

This vinaigrette will keep in the refrigerator for 12 days.

FALL APPLE SLAW

SERVES 4 TO 6

⅓ cup cider vinegar

2 tablespoons whole grain mustard

2 tablespoons apple cider

1 tablespoon honey

Kosher salt, to taste

Black pepper, to taste

1 tablespoon extra virgin olive oil

2 apples (1 green and 1 red), cored and thinly sliced

½ head savoy cabbage (about 1 pound), peeled, cored, and thinly sliced

2 kohlrabi (about 1 pound), peeled, cored, and cut into matchsticks

1 stalk celery, thinly sliced

½ cup Pickled Red Onions (pg. 222)

3 tablespoons chopped parsley

½ pound brussels sprouts, trimmed and thinly sliced

In a large bowl, whisk together the vinegar, mustard, apple cider, honey, and a pinch of salt and pepper. Slowly whisk in olive oil to incorporate.

Fold in the apples, cabbage, kohlrabi, celery, Pickled Red Onions, parsley, and brussels sprouts. Season to taste with salt and pepper.

Refrigerate for at least 2 hours to allow flavors to meld. Serve alongside grilled pork chops or use on sandwiches.

This slaw will keep in the refrigerator for 1 week.

SPROUTS

IF there were ever a crop that surprised us with its rapid gain in popularity, it must be brussels sprouts. Even kale, the vegetable darling of the last few years, has seen a slower adoption rate. In the early 2000s, we would still have to talk our customers—outside of those few in the know—into trying sprouts. This sometimes meant standing next to the brimming bushel basket and giving cooking tips while promising they weren't as harsh as many people remembered. Since then, they have taken a rightful and ubiquitous seasonal spot on menus and in home kitchens everywhere. We start to pick them in earnest in early September, but diehard fans swear they taste even sweeter after the first nip of frost. Once the weather cools off a bit, we jump from picking a bushel a week to a bushel a day. As Thanksgiving approaches, we could spend all day picking them off their Dr. Seuss-like stalks and still not meet the demand.

SPROUT KRAUT

Near the end of the growing season, when a harsh frost is on its way, we become inundated with brussels sprouts. In addition to roasting, braising, and sautéing them, we love making this versatile condiment. It goes on everything from salads to sausage and is a great way to mix up your sprout game. Think of it as a New Englander's approach to sauerkraut.

MAKES 3 CUPS

¼ teaspoon caraway seed

1½ pounds brussels sprouts

⅓ cup shredded carrots

2 scallions, chopped

½ teaspoon fresh horseradish, chopped

1½ tablespoons kosher salt

Black pepper, to taste

Toast caraway seeds in a dry skillet over medium heat until they become brown and fragrant, about 2 minutes. Let cool. Grind into a fine powder.

Trim and thinly slice the brussel sprouts. Place the ground caraway seeds, the sliced sprouts, and the remaining ingredients in a large bowl and, using your hands, thoroughly mix.

Press the sprouts so they release their water, then taste. The sprouts should be salty but not overwhelmingly so. Adjust seasoning if necessary.

After a few minutes, the sprouts should look limp and brine will begin pooling in the bowl. Let sit for 10 minutes, then massage by hand for a few more minutes. Transfer mixture to a crock or glass jar.

Using your hand, push the vegetables down hard, releasing any air bubbles and making sure the vegetables are completely submerged. If necessary, add more water to cover, leaving at least an inch of space at the top of the container.

Place an open food storage bag into the container with the top of the bag extending beyond the mouth of the crock or jar. Fill the bag with water, ensuring the bottom of the bag makes full contact with the brine solution underneath. This water bag will act as a weight to keep the mixture submerged and clean while allowing air to escape during the fermentation process.

Store the kraut at room temperature out of direct sunlight for about 5 days. Taste; it should be sour with a soft texture, as if it has been cooked. Let sit another 2 to 4 days if you want more tang.

This kraut will keep in a sealed container in the refrigerator for up to 6 months.

ESCAROLE KIMCHI

MAKES ABOUT 4 CUPS

2 heads escarole
(about 1¾ pounds)

¼ cup kosher salt

2 tablespoons chopped ginger

1 tablespoon chopped garlic

2 tablespoons Korean chili
paste (or 2 tablespoons
chili flakes)

1 teaspoon granulated sugar

½ teaspoon fish sauce

¼ pound radishes, halved
and thinly sliced

⅓ cup shredded carrots

½ cup chopped scallions

Core and chop the escarole into bite-size pieces. In a bowl, mix together escarole and salt, gently massaging by hand so that the salt evenly coats escarole.

Add enough water to just cover escarole and let sit for 30 minutes. Drain and reserve 1 cup brine.

In a separate bowl, mix together the ginger, garlic, chili paste or flakes, sugar, and fish sauce. Add the escarole, radishes, carrots, and scallions and mix thoroughly. Transfer to a crock or glass jar. Using your hand, push the vegetables down hard, releasing any air bubbles and making sure the vegetables are completely submerged. Add enough reserved brine to cover, leaving at least an inch of space at the top of the container.

Place an open food storage bag into the container with the top of the bag extending beyond the mouth of the crock or jar. Fill the bag with water, ensuring the bottom of the bag makes full contact with the brine solution underneath. This water bag will act as a weight to keep the mixture submerged and clean while allowing air to escape during the fermentation process.

Store the kimchi at room temperature out of direct sunlight for about 5 days. Taste; it should be sour with a soft texture, as if it has been cooked. Let sit another 2 to 4 days if you want more tang.

This kimchi will keep in a sealed container in the refrigerator for up to 6 months.

BAKED PASTA *with* SAUSAGE *and* SWISS CHARD PESTO

1 pound penne pasta

2 tablespoons olive oil

1 pound sweet Italian sausage

1 small yellow onion,
thinly sliced

½ pint grape tomatoes, halved

1 recipe Swiss Chard Pesto

¾ cup shaved Asiago cheese,
divided

Kosher salt, to taste

Black pepper, to taste

Preheat oven to 350°F.

Cook pasta according to package directions but drain two minutes before done. Rinse with cold water and set aside.

Heat olive oil in a large pan over medium-high heat. Remove and discard sausage casings, add sausage, and brown the meat, breaking it up until it is cooked and crumbly, about 10 to 12 minutes. Remove sausage from pan and set aside.

Add onions to the pot and brown, about 10 to 12 minutes. Remove from heat and drain fat. Add tomatoes and scrape up any bits of sausage and onions stuck to the bottom of the pan.

Lightly grease a baking dish with butter or cooking spray. In the prepared baking dish, combine onion and tomato mixture with sausage, pasta, Swiss Chard Pesto, and ½ cup cheese, and season to taste with salt and pepper. Sprinkle remaining cheese on top and bake in the oven until golden and bubbly, about 20 to 25 minutes.

Serve hot from the pan.

SWISS CHARD PESTO

½ cup grated Asiago cheese

¼ cup toasted walnuts

1 large garlic clove

Kosher salt, to taste

Black pepper, to taste

2 cups packed Swiss
chard leaves

¼ cup basil

¼ cup parsley leaves

1½ tablespoons chopped sage

¼ cup extra virgin olive oil

Put cheese, walnuts, garlic, and a pinch of salt and pepper into a food processor and pulse for 20 seconds. Add the Swiss chard and pulse for 10 seconds.

Add basil, parsley, and sage, pulse for 20 seconds, then scrape down sides.

With processor running, slowly pour in olive oil until combined. Season to taste with salt and pepper.

This pesto will keep in the refrigerator for 5 days.

ZUCCHINI *and* TOMATOES

This dish was a staple of summer lunch breaks when we were growing up. Our grandfather would throw all the ingredients into a slow cooker at dawn and go about his work. By lunch, we'd be chowing down on this dish with obscene amounts of bread on the side.

Like many of his dishes, the success of such simple preparation rests entirely on the quality of the ingredients. It seems fitting that a true farmer's lunch should be easy to prepare; the hard work of growing the ingredients is already done.

SERVES 4 TO 6

6 pounds plum tomatoes, cored and chopped

4 medium zucchini (about 3½ pounds), sliced

1 medium Spanish onion, chopped

½ cup olive oil

3 tablespoons chopped garlic

½ bunch parsley

½ bunch basil

Kosher salt, to taste

Black pepper, to taste

Place tomatoes, zucchini, onions, olive oil, garlic, and parsley into a crockpot or large stock pot. Cook on low for 5 to 6 hours, stirring occasionally. Add basil 10 minutes prior to serving. Season to taste with salt and pepper.

Serve warm with a good loaf of Italian bread.

ZUCCHINI AND SUMMER SQUASH

OF the wide variety of summer squash we grow, zucchini rules the roost. Other varieties like the UFO-shaped patty pans, the mild and tender Cousa, and the classic yellow squash all have loyal adherents, but the love for zucchini remains constant. Luckily, zucchini is also prolific.

We grow three summer squash crops each season and expect to pick the crop for about a month each. As the plants grow and spread, fertilizer and water are provided by drip irrigation right at the roots. This keeps the foliage dry and healthy. The flowers start to open a few weeks after planting, attracting bees with their wide, golden blooms. Each plant gives a fruit every day or so, and we harvest them daily. They grow very quickly in the heat of summer when the nights stay warm. We like to catch them before they get too big so that they are tender throughout.

The crew about to unload a truckload of Christmas trees, 1998.

THE farm was built with sweat and sacrifice by a diverse labor force. Farm work in the early years was a physically demanding job, with most (if not all) labor done by hand, seven days a week during the peak seasons. The days were long and the pay short but sorely needed for the new immigrants trying to get a foothold in America. Among the Italian immigrants were the Socci brothers and Mr. Farina, both from the hill towns of the Apennine mountains near Atina. Tony Angelucci was another key Italian native who later became a produce manager for Star Market. His family now owns Russell Farms in Woburn.

After the war, when Margie opened up the farmstand, more job opportunities requiring less strenuous work became available. Arthur Halliday moved into the retail operation as a produce manager. Mary, Viola, and Jenny Carrusso were sisters from Nonantum and Watertown who began working in the farmstand. They all moved to the Needham stand in 1962. When Margie fell ill and Anne began working less than the usual seventy-hour weeks, Mary became farmstand manager in the late 1960s. After the crash in the farm's labor force in 1973, we began rebuilding and hired Martin Dzengeleski. He was our farm manager for more than twenty years before he left for a higher calling and was ordained as a Catholic priest.

Upon Martin's departure, Lee took up the slack without missing a beat. Lee's sister Lynne began working at the farm a few years prior to Lee's employment. Hired as a greenhouse manager, she soon took on a multitude of responsibilities and quickly became an integral part of the farm. The more challenges she faced, the more Lynne excelled.

The farm was and is the first job for many local kids. Twenty years ago, a man told me a story about working for my grandfather in the 1930s when he was thirteen. He oversaw the irrigation and slowly turned the pipes all night long to water the crops evenly. He spoke to me of Peter and how he had taught him to work. His modest income was a great help to his struggling family during the Depression. We could fill another book with the multitude of people who have had their first jobs here. There were many who helped build the farm into what it is today.

– Al Volante

Clockwise from top left: Pastry chef Jen Heberlein plating dessert, 2016; the Newton crew, 1930s; Alena at Dinner in the Field, 2016; Carrie with samples of heirloom tomatoes, 2011; Ryan Conroy in the zinnias, 2000s; Molly moving pumpkins, 1980s. Center top to bottom: Field manager Lee, 2016; Lefty and Robert picking beans, 2010.

THE FARM FAMILY OVER THE YEARS

A family farm like ours relies on a crew dedicated to efficiently cultivating the finest quality crops—a crew that is willing to do the hard work to deliver the produce from the field to the customer. This timeline is an overview of the farm crew throughout the years.

1920s Peter picked up Italian day laborers in Nonantum to do the bulk of the farm's daily work. By the late 1920s, the farm was poised to weather the Great Depression relatively well, in large part due to the available hands in the neighborhood.

1930s In the late 1930s and into the 1940s, Peter's Florida-based crew traveled north to work summers in Newton before returning south for the winter with Peter's equipment to work his fields there.

1940s During World War II, able bodies were extremely scarce with so many men fighting overseas. For a time, German prisoners of war were brought over to American soil and some worked Peter's Newton fields.

1950s In the 1950s, the crew was comprised of seasonal employees. Jamaicans, Puerto Ricans, and Peter and Ferdinand's friends from Italy traveled to Newton for work.

1960s When the farm moved with Ferdinand and Anne to Needham, several loyal workers made the shift as well, applying their skills toward the opening of the new stand.

1970s When Al took over operations in 1972, he employed local kids since the migrant population was not reliably present in these years. He tried hiring groups of Native Americans from Maine and Mexican Americans from the south, but these crews never found their stride.

1980s Seasonal Jamaican laborers worked their first summer in 1988. The crew included Colman Jones, who has been at the farm ever since. Like Colman, much of the current field crew is from Jamaica and has been with the farm for a decade or more.

1990s to 2000s About a dozen members of today's farmstand crew arrived in the 1990s and early 2000s. This crew worked with three generations of the farm all at once—Ferdinand, Al, and his children. The current generation of Volantes grew up watching them and learning from them.

2010s The scope of the farm is now beyond field, greenhouse, and retail. The year-round nature of the business has led to the largest increase in staffing yet for this century-old farm. With the kitchen and expanded food service, the farm has labor needs like never before.

1920s & 1930s

1960s

1960s

VOLANTE FARM

1980s

1990s

1990s

1990s

1990s

2000s

EARLY FALL VEGETABLE CURRY

SERVES 4 TO 6

2 medium carrots
(about ½ pound)

⅓ pound Yukon Gold potatoes

1 medium eggplant

1 small red onion

1 small red bell pepper

1½ pounds tomatoes

¼ pound green beans

½ head cauliflower
(about ¾ pound)

½ pound collard greens

¼ cup olive oil, divided

2 tablespoons chopped garlic

2 tablespoons peeled and
chopped ginger

2 teaspoons Garam Masala
(pg. 227)

Kosher salt, to taste

1 15-ounce can coconut milk

1 tablespoon lime juice

Chili flakes, to taste (optional)

Prepare the vegetables. Peel and thinly slice the carrots. Dice the potatoes, eggplant, onion, and bell pepper. Core and chop the tomatoes. Remove and discard the stems from the green beans and cut the beans in half. Cut the cauliflower into bite-size pieces. Remove the stems from the collard greens and cut them into bite-size pieces.

Heat half of the olive oil in a large pot over medium-high heat. Add carrots and lightly brown, about 4 to 5 minutes. Remove and set aside. Add cauliflower and lightly brown, about 4 to 5 minutes, then remove and set aside separate from the carrots. Add potatoes and lightly brown, about 8 to 10 minutes. Remove and set aside with cauliflower.

Add remaining olive oil to pan. Add eggplant and cook for 5 minutes. Add onions and cook for 10 minutes, stirring frequently. Add garlic and ginger and cook for another 3 minutes, adjusting heat if necessary to prevent burning. Add Garam Masala and a pinch of salt and cook until fragrant, about 30 seconds. Add tomatoes and cook for 15 minutes. The eggplant should essentially dissolve into the mixture, thickening it along the way.

Add coconut milk and simmer for 8 minutes. Stir in potatoes and cauliflower and simmer for 7 minutes. Add carrots, green beans, bell pepper, and collard greens and simmer for 10 minutes longer, until vegetables are al dente. Remove pot from heat and stir in lime juice and chili flakes (if using). Season to taste with salt and serve over hot basmati rice.

LAST *of the* TOMATOES BREAD PUDDING

The last of the tomatoes need not be a tragedy. As the season comes to a close, tomatoes become less frequent, but the cool nights can really add to their sweetness. This dish is a way to enjoy the last fresh tomatoes of the year as a perfect comfort food.

SERVES 4 TO 6

1½ pounds tomatoes, cored and halved

2 tablespoons salted butter

1 small yellow onion, diced

1 fennel bulb, diced

1 tablespoon chopped garlic

1 yellow bell pepper, deseeded and diced

1 teaspoon chopped fresh savory

1 teaspoon kosher salt, plus more to taste

Pinch of black pepper

1½ cups mascarpone cheese

2 eggs, beaten

8½ cups diced crusty bread

¼ cup chopped basil

1½ cups grated Asiago cheese, divided

Squeeze out juice and seeds from tomatoes. Cut into bite-size pieces and place in a colander to drain.

Melt butter in a large sauté pan over medium-high heat. Add onions and fennel and cook until golden brown, about 10 to 12 minutes. Add garlic and cook for 2 minutes, then add tomatoes and cook for 5 minutes. Add bell pepper and cook for 2 minutes. Add savory, one teaspoon of salt, and a pinch of pepper, remove from heat, and let cool completely.

Preheat oven to 375°F.

In a large mixing bowl, whisk together the mascarpone, eggs, and a pinch of salt and pepper. Then add cooled vegetable mixture, bread, basil, and half of the Asiago cheese. Mix gently until combined and pour into a greased 9-by-13-inch baking dish. Bake in oven for 15 minutes.

After 15 minutes, sprinkle remaining cheese on top and increase the oven temperature to 400°F. Bake until golden brown and bubbly, about 10 to 15 minutes more. Serve alongside grilled chicken and a simple salad.

GRILLED CORNETTAS

Every winter we scour seed catalogs for new and interesting vegetable varieties, but one we never need to replace is our very own Mr. Volante's Cornetta Pepper.

Ferdinand Volante brought this pepper over from Italy. It is a slender red pepper with a shape reminiscent of its spicy cousin, the Hot Portugal. However, hot it is not. In fact, it is one of the sweetest peppers out there. The peppers ripen in clusters, with each plant producing dozens in a season. We harvest the first two ripened bushels of Cornettas every year for our personal seed stores.

Ferdinand used to collect, dry, and save the seeds from these peppers himself. The true highlight of this tradition is not just in the seeding, but in the aftermath. After he got all the seeds out, Ferdinand would grill up the Cornettas and bring them to us, still oily and warm, on a cold fall morning before the stand opened. Often he would just lean out the open window of his pickup, waving a tinfoil packet of them at whomever he saw. The staff would scoop up the peppers and shove them into hot loaves of Italian bread for an early snack. We all looked forward to this tasty tradition year after year. "A little oil, a little salt, a little garlic" was the only recipe we ever got. The secret is in knowing that, to Ferdinand, nothing was ever "a little."

Since his passing, one of our field crewmembers, Lefty, does the arduous cutting, coring, cleaning, and deseeding to make sure we have peppers the following year—and we still cook them up for the staff's coffee break the next day.

– Ryan Conroy

SERVES WHOMEVER IS FASTEST

3 tablespoons olive oil

2 pounds Cornetta peppers, halved and deseeded

1 tablespoon kosher salt

3 tablespoons chopped garlic (optional)*

1 loaf crusty Italian bread or baguette

while the 3 tablespoons are optional, 6 is definitely preferred

Cover grill grates with foil and preheat grill to high.

In a bowl, drizzle olive oil over peppers, sprinkle with salt, and mix thoroughly. Add garlic if desired.

When grill is hot, dump peppers onto foil and spread into a single layer. Cover and cook until they develop a good char, about 3 to 5 minutes.

Flip the peppers, cover, and cook until they look like they are starting to melt, another 3 to 5 minutes.

Remove from grill and pile onto a plate. Tear chunks off of loaf and stuff peppers into chunks. Best enjoyed before 7 a.m.

ROAST PORK *with* AUTUMN STUFFING

SERVES 6

2 tablespoons olive oil

½ cup diced bacon
(about 3 slices)

2 medium yellow onions
(about 1 pound), thinly sliced

1 tablespoon chopped garlic

½ cup Madeira wine

½ cup apple cider

3 tablespoons chopped sage

Kosher salt, to taste

Black pepper, to taste

4 ounces baby arugula

3 pounds pork loin roast

1 Fuji apple, peeled, cored,
and thinly sliced

Butcher's twine

Heat olive oil in a large sauté pan over medium-high heat. Add bacon and cook until golden brown, about 6 to 8 minutes. Remove and set aside. Add onions to pan and cook, stirring as little as possible, for about 10 minutes. Lower heat to medium-low and continue cooking until onions are completely caramelized, about 18 to 20 minutes more.

Increase heat to medium-high and add garlic. Cook for 2 minutes, then add wine and cook until completely absorbed, about 6 to 8 minutes. Add cider and cook for another 8 to 10 minutes.

Remove from heat, add sage, and season to taste with salt and pepper. Transfer to a bowl, let cool, and fold in arugula.

Preheat oven to 375°F.

Place pork on a cutting board and butterfly. Cut the length of the pork loin parallel to the cutting board about ½-inch from the underside of the loin but do not cut through. Unroll the top of the loin as you would a roll of paper towels so that you end up with one complete flat piece.

Season inside of pork with salt and pepper, then spread onion mixture all over inside of pork, leaving a 1-inch border. Top with apple slices and then roll pork back up. Tie the pork roll with butcher's twine, with 1 piece along the length of the loin and 6 to 8 pieces across.

Season the outside of pork with salt and pepper.

Roast pork in the oven until the internal temperature reaches 135°F to 145°F, about 60 to 75 minutes.

Remove from oven and let rest for 10 minutes. Discard twine and slice pork into 1-inch pieces. Serve with roasted potatoes and a dollop of Rhubarb and Thyme Jam (pg. 40).

SCALLOPS *on* SPICED CABBAGE *with* PEAS *and* CARROTS

In the spring, the pea harvest can be overwhelming, so we turn to the freezer to help us contain all those sweet, green morsels. Anyone on the farm with idle time (sorry, ice cream scoopers) is never without their personal bushel of peapods. Hour after hour, we make our way through the arduous task of shelling the peas for freezing.

It's tedious work, but it certainly pays off when you can put homegrown peas into a fall or winter meal like this one.

SERVES 4 TO 6

SPICED CABBAGE

2 carrots (about ½ pound)

2½ tablespoons salted butter, divided

1 tablespoon chopped garlic

1 tablespoon chopped ginger

2 tablespoons diced shallots

½ teaspoon Garam Masala (pg. 227)

1 15-ounce can coconut milk

½ head savoy cabbage, cut into 1-inch squares

1 cup shelled peas

Kosher salt, to taste

1½ teaspoons lime juice

1 tablespoon chopped parsley

1 teaspoon chopped mint

SCALLOPS

2 pounds fresh scallops, side muscles removed

Kosher salt, to taste

Black pepper, to taste

4 tablespoons olive oil, divided

Make spiced cabbage. Peel and cut the carrots into thin rounds. Melt 1½ tablespoons butter in a large, wide-bottomed pot over medium heat. Add carrots and cook until they begin to brown, about 8 to 10 minutes. Add garlic, ginger, and shallots and cook for 1 minute. Add Garam Masala and cook for 30 seconds. Add coconut milk and simmer for 4 minutes.

Add cabbage to pan and cook until almost wilted, about 8 to 10 minutes. Add peas and a pinch of salt and cook for 2 minutes.

Remove from heat and stir in remaining butter, lime juice, parsley, and mint. Season to taste with salt, set aside, and cover to keep warm.

Cook scallops. Pat scallops dry with paper towels. Season both sides with salt and pepper. Heat 2 tablespoons olive oil in a large sauté pan over high heat. Add half of the scallops and cook until brown on one side, about 2 minutes. Flip and cook for another 30 seconds, then remove from pan. Wipe pan clean and repeat with remaining olive oil and scallops.

Serve seared scallops immediately over spiced cabbage.

SHORT RIB STUFFED PEPPERS

SERVES 4 TO 6

1½ teaspoons dried oregano

¼ teaspoon ground cumin

¼ teaspoon ground coriander

¼ teaspoon ground cinnamon

¼ teaspoon ground cloves

¼ teaspoon paprika

Pinch of cayenne pepper

2 pounds short ribs

Kosher salt, to taste

Black pepper, to taste

9 tablespoons olive oil, divided

1 cup red wine

1½ quarts beef stock

1½ pounds plum tomatoes

3 large assorted bell peppers

1 medium yellow onion, diced

2 tablespoons chopped garlic

1 ounce Mexican chocolate (such as Taza)

1½ cups fresh corn kernels (about 2 ears)

¾ cup cooked pinto beans

1 cup crumbled queso fresco

1 tablespoon Delfino cilantro

Preheat oven to 325°F.

In a small bowl, mix together the oregano, cumin, coriander, cinnamon, cloves, paprika, and cayenne pepper. Season the short ribs with the spice mix and a few pinches of salt and pepper.

Heat 3 tablespoons olive oil in a large ovenproof pot over medium-high heat. When the olive oil is smoking, gently place the ribs in the pot and brown evenly on each side, about 3 minutes per side. When browned all over, remove from pot and set aside. Remove and discard all remaining olive oil from pot.

Return pot to stove on medium-high heat and add wine. Reduce by half, about 4 to 5 minutes. Add stock and bring to boil. Add short ribs back to pot, cover, and transfer pot to oven. Cook until tender, about 2½ to 3 hours. When ribs are done, gently remove from pot and let cool. Skim and discard any fat and set short ribs aside. Reserve 1 cup liquid.

Increase oven temperature to 400°F.

Core the tomatoes and bell peppers and cut them in half lengthwise, keeping them separate.

Lightly coat tomatoes with 2 tablespoons olive oil and a pinch of salt and pepper. Repeat with bell peppers. Roast tomatoes on a sheet pan for 15 minutes. Add the peppers and roast until tomato skins are brown and peppers are halfway cooked, about 8 to 10 minutes. Set aside peppers. Skin the tomatoes, discard the peels, chop the tomatoes, and set aside.

Heat 2 tablespoons olive oil in a large sauté pan over medium-high heat. Add onions and cook until golden brown, about 10 to 12 minutes. Add garlic and cook for 1 minute. Add tomatoes and cook for 5 minutes.

Add 1 cup reserved short rib liquid and simmer for 10 minutes. Remove from heat and stir in chocolate pieces, then season to taste with salt and pepper.

Cut short ribs into bite-size pieces and combine with tomato mixture in a large mixing bowl. Add corn, beans, queso fresco, and cilantro. Mix together and season to taste with salt and pepper. Stuff mixture into peppers, place peppers on a sheet pan, and roast for 10 minutes.

Remove from oven and serve hot with a small amount of reserved short rib liquid drizzled on top.

RYAN'S FERMENTED HOT SAUCE

Volante Farms' field manager Ryan Conroy becomes immensely popular during the holiday season thanks to his enviable hot sauce recipe, which he makes in large batches toward the end of harvest season. He cycles a batch through his one-gallon fermenting crock every two weeks, then combines the batches to create his special holiday blend.

This recipe can be easily scaled up or down depending on the size of your holiday crowd. Any homegrown hot pepper will work, but red cayenne, serrano, and jalapeños give amazing color and have plenty of flavor and heat. Using homegrown peppers is essential, as peppers found in most grocery stores may have been irradiated for storage, a process that significantly hinders successful fermentation.

4 teaspoons sea salt

1 quart room-temperature water

3 to 5 cloves garlic, peeled

½ medium yellow onion, roughly chopped

1 pound assorted ripe hot peppers, stems removed

½ cup white balsamic or rice vinegar

SAFETY NOTE: Touching hot peppers with your bare hands can lead to a world of unpleasantness as the oil can linger, even after washing your hands thoroughly. Blending and processing even a small batch of hot peppers can release enough capsaicin-laced vapor to irritate your eyes and sinuses. To prevent the vapors from affecting you, make sure your kitchen is well ventilated (open windows and/or crank your stove's hood), wear gloves, and consider blending your hot sauce outside. Keep that immersion blender in the cabinet for this recipe; you don't want to get splashed.

Before you place the peppers into the fermentation container, make sure to clean it thoroughly.

Dissolve sea salt in the water and set aside the brine.

Smash garlic cloves to release their oils, drop them in the bottom of a fermenting crock or quart jar, and add onions.

Slice 4 largest peppers in half and set aside. Chop remaining peppers into 1-inch pieces, stuff them into the crock or jar, and top with halved peppers to prevent diced pieces from floating to the surface. Leave at least an inch of space between the peppers and lip of container.

Add enough brine to cover the peppers. Place an open food storage bag into the container with the top of the bag extending beyond the mouth of the crock or jar. Fill the bag with water, ensuring the bottom makes full contact with the brine underneath. This water bag acts as a weight to keep the mixture submerged and clean while allowing air to escape during the fermentation process.

Place container in a cool, dark place for 2 weeks. During this time, bubbles will rise through the mixture. A pasty-white or cream-colored yeast may form in the jar. The yeast growth won't hurt the final product, but it can be slowed by adding 1/2 teaspoon of sea salt to the jar and re-sealing it. If green and blue mold begins to grow in the jar, the hot sauce has spoiled; throw it away. If nothing has happened after a week, add a teaspoon of raw sugar or a splash of white wine to the jar.

After 2 weeks of fermentation, strain the peppers and reserve the brine.

Put on gloves. Transfer the peppers to blender and pulse until they are the consistency of mashed potatoes. If necessary, add some of the reserved brine to help the peppers liquefy. Once the mixture is blended, run the peppers through a food mill to remove any seeds.

The resulting sauce can be used in this concentrated form, like Sriracha. To achieve a more classic consistency, combine 1 part white balsamic or rice vinegar with 2 parts hot pepper mixture. Simmer this combination on the stove for a few minutes to help it emulsify. Do not inhale the steam.

This hot sauce will keep in a sealed container in the refrigerator for up to 1 year.

RUSTIC APPLE TART

MAKES ONE 9-INCH TART

CRUST

1 cup all-purpose flour

3 tablespoons fine cornmeal

1 tablespoon granulated sugar

¼ teaspoon iodized salt

6 tablespoons unsalted butter, cubed, cold

3 tablespoons sour cream

2 tablespoons cold water

FILLING

1 egg

1 teaspoon milk

2 firm baking apples, such as Cortland

¼ cup Apple Sauce (pg. 196)

¼ cup turbinado sugar

Make dough for crust. Place flour, cornmeal, sugar, and salt in the bowl of a food processor. Add butter and pulse until the mixture resembles a coarse meal, about 10 to 15 times. Dump into a large bowl. Add sour cream and water and mix to combine. Dough should not be sticky but should come together when pressed with your hands. If crumbly, add a little more water; if too wet, add flour.

Press dough into a flattened disc, wrap in plastic, and refrigerate for 15 to 20 minutes.

Line a baking sheet with parchment paper and preheat oven to 400°F

Lightly flour a large work surface and roll dough into a 12-inch circle. Transfer to prepared baking sheet. Cover with plastic and refrigerate for at least 10 minutes and up to 24 hours.

While dough is in the refrigerator, whisk the egg and milk together until combined, then set aside. Peel, core, and slice apples into ¼-inch-thick slices. Set aside.

Remove dough from refrigerator. Spread a thin layer of Apple Sauce over dough, leaving a 1-inch border around the edge. Arrange apple slices in overlapping circles, starting at the edge of the Apple Sauce and working toward the middle, maintaining the 1-inch border around the edge.

Fold the border of the dough over the outside edges of the apples and, using a pastry brush, brush the dough with egg wash. Sprinkle the entire tart liberally with sugar.

Bake for 15 minutes. Rotate pan, then bake until browned and crispy on top, another 10 to 15 minutes. To check doneness, slide a spatula under the bottom of the tart to see if it is golden brown as well. If it browns too much after the first 15 minutes, reduce heat to 350°F and continue baking as instructed.

Cool to room temperature and serve with vanilla ice cream or whipped cream.

APPLES

OUR trusted growers take great care in their orchards, ensuring we have plenty of apples perfect for every purpose. There are baking apples, snacking apples, saucing apples, old favorites, and modern hybrids. Crowd favorites like Honeycrisp and Macoun are necessary, of course. Plenty of variety exists beyond these, like heirlooms with a taste and look of yesteryear, such as American Beauty or Golden Russet. With thousands of known varieties and hundreds worth tasting, we seek greater availability every year. This variety adds spice to life in the fall.

APPLE SAUCE

MAKES 4 TO 6 CUPS

6 McIntosh apples (about 3 pounds)

1 cup apple cider

1 cinnamon stick

Pinch of kosher salt

1 tablespoon lemon juice

2 tablespoons brown sugar, plus more to taste

½ teaspoon ground cinnamon

Peel, core, and cut apples into eighths. Place apples, cider, cinnamon stick, salt, and lemon juice in a non-aluminum saucepan. Bring to a boil then reduce heat and simmer for 20 minutes, stirring occasionally.

Stir in brown sugar and cinnamon, then cook until apples are mushy and sauce has thickened, about 10 more minutes. Add brown sugar to taste.

Remove from heat and discard cinnamon stick. Serve warm or cold.

The texture is variable; the sauce can be mashed with a potato masher or fork to make it chunkier or processed in a blender for a smoother, more uniform consistency.

This apple sauce will keep in the refrigerator for up to 1 week and in the freezer for 6 months.

PUMPKIN CHOCOLATE CHIP BROWNIES

BROWNIES

1 small sugar pumpkin
(about 3 pounds)

1½ cups all-purpose flour

¾ teaspoon baking powder

½ teaspoon iodized salt

8 tablespoons unsalted
butter, melted

½ cup vegetable oil

1¾ cups granulated sugar

1 tablespoon vanilla extract

2 eggs

¼ cup unsweetened
cocoa powder

½ cup semi-sweet mini
chocolate chips

1 teaspoon ground cinnamon

⅛ teaspoon ground cloves

½ teaspoon ground nutmeg

½ teaspoon ground ginger

TOPPING

½ cup roasted pepitas

¼ cup brown sugar

1 tablespoon all-purpose flour

Pinch of iodized salt

½ teaspoon ground cinnamon

1 tablespoon unsalted butter,
melted

¼ cup semi-sweet mini
chocolate chips

Grease a 9-by-13-inch baking dish and preheat oven to 350°F.

Slice pumpkin into quarters. Remove seeds and place slices skin side down on a sheet pan. Roast in the oven until tender, about 45 to 60 minutes. Time will vary greatly depending on thickness and size of pumpkin slices.

Remove pumpkin from oven, let cool for 5 minutes, peel pumpkin slices, and discard skins. Purée pumpkin flesh using a food processor or blender, strain, and reserve 2/3 cup pumpkin purée. Freeze the rest for a pie or your next batch of brownies (purée will keep in the freezer for up to 6 months).

Prepare topping. In a bowl, stir together pepitas, brown sugar, flour, salt, and cinnamon. Pour melted butter over top and stir. When mixture is completely cool, stir in chocolate chips. Set aside.

Prepare brownies. In a bowl, stir together flour, baking powder, and salt and set aside.

In another bowl, stir together the melted butter, oil, sugar, and vanilla extract. Whisk in eggs 1 at a time. Stir in flour mixture to form batter. Divide batter in half and separate into 2 bowls.

Add cocoa and chocolate chips to first bowl of batter, combine thoroughly, and set aside. Add puréed pumpkin, cinnamon, cloves, nutmeg, and ginger to the second bowl and mix until pumpkin is evenly incorporated throughout the batter.

Spread the chocolate batter in the bottom of the pan and spread the pumpkin batter on top of the chocolate layer. Drag a skewer, toothpick, or knife tip through the layers, swirling them gently together. Sprinkle evenly with topping.

Bake until brownies begin to pull away from the sides of the baking dish and a toothpick inserted into the center comes out with moist crumbs, about 40 minutes. Remove from oven, cool to room temperature, and enjoy!

CONCORD GRAPE TARTS

MAKES 12 TO 16 TARTS

TART SHELLS

1½ cups all-purpose flour

⅓ cup granulated sugar

¼ teaspoon iodized salt

1¼ teaspoons baking powder

8 tablespoons salted butter, cubed, cold

2 tablespoons lemon zest

1 teaspoon vanilla extract

2 tablespoons water

1 egg

FILLING

5½ cups ripe Concord grapes

2 tablespoons instant tapioca

1 cup granulated sugar

TOPPING

1½ cups rolled oats

1 cup all-purpose flour

¾ cup light brown sugar

½ teaspoon iodized salt

8 tablespoons unsalted butter, melted

Make tart shell dough. Place flour, sugar, salt, baking powder, butter, and lemon zest in a food processor. Pulse until mixture resembles small peas.

Transfer to a bowl, add vanilla extract, water, and egg, and knead into a ball. Refrigerate dough for at least 1 hour (dough can be made a day ahead).

Make the filling. Rinse grapes and pop the pulp (insides) out of grape skins and into a heavy-bottomed, non-aluminum saucepan. Reserve skins in a separate bowl. Combine tapioca and sugar with skins.

Boil pulp for about 5 minutes, stirring often to keep from burning. Skim foam off the top as needed.

Remove pulp from heat and strain over bowl of skins. Press on pulp to release as much juice as possible. Discard pulp and seeds then stir skin and juice mixture. Refrigerate mixture for at least 2 hours.

Assemble the topping. In a bowl, stir all ingredients together until combined. Set aside until ready to use.

Preheat oven to 325°F.

Grease a muffin pan with butter or cooking spray. Remove dough from refrigerator and roll it out until it is 1/4-inch thick. Cut out circles that are about 1 inch larger than the circumference of the muffin cavity and gently press each into prepared muffin pan. Freeze for at least 10 minutes or until ready to use. (If you don't freeze them, the tart shells will shrink when baked.) When ready to bake, place the muffin pan on a sheet pan to catch any filling that bubbles over.

Fill tarts almost to the top with cooled grape filling. Cover each with a tablespoon of oat topping. Bake until bubbling, 25 to 30 minutes.

Cool completely before unmolding. Serve at room temperature.

HOT PEPPER DAIQUIRI

Tim Grejtak

Daiquiris, classic drinks with origins in naval history, follow the fundamental structure of most cocktails: two parts spirit, one part sugar, and one part citrus. One of the advantages of such a basic structure is that daiquiri recipes are very malleable.

In order to bring this nautical cocktail ashore to Volante Farms, we infused a simple syrup with spicy, earthy, gingery notes from parsnips and the farm's own hot peppers. By simmering these ingredients in a mixture of water and sugar, more complex flavor compounds that would otherwise remain trapped in the vegetables are drawn out.

The resulting cocktail evokes warm Indian summers and crisp autumn evenings, perfect for dinner parties and nights by the fire pit.

MAKES 1 DRINK

PARSNIP/HOT PEPPER SYRUP
MAKES 8 OUNCES

1 cup granulated sugar

1 cup water

1 cup packed grated parsnips (about 2 parsnips)

1 serrano pepper, halved, seeds and ribs retained

COCKTAIL

2 ounces light Jamaican rum

¾ ounce lime juice

1 ounce Parsnip/Hot Pepper Syrup

GARNISH

1 thinly sliced apple wedge

Prepare syrup. In medium saucepan over high heat, bring sugar, water, and grated parsnips to a boil and cook until sugar dissolves. Cover, lower heat, and simmer for 45 minutes, stirring occasionally.

Strain grated parsnip into heatproof bowl, pressing out remaining syrup from parsnip pulp. Return strained syrup to the saucepan, add halved pepper, and simmer approximately 2 minutes. The longer it simmers, the spicier it will be, so taste syrup every minute or so. Aim for an intense spice; don't worry—it will be diluted in the cocktail.

Strain out hot pepper and set syrup aside until cool. Parsnip/Hot Pepper Syrup will keep in the refrigerator for up to 1 month.

Make the daiquiri. Shake the rum, lime juice, and Parsnip/Hot Pepper Syrup with ice in cocktail shaker for 30 seconds. Strain into a chilled cocktail glass and garnish with apple wedge.

Dave, Teri, and Steve, 2016.

VOLANTE FARMS
— Winter —
DAVE, TERI & STEVE

Clockwise from top left: Dave in the cornstalks, 1990s; family portrait, 1980s; Teri bunching snapdragons, 2010; family portrait at Standish, 2000; Steve plowing the Standish fields, 2000.

NEEDHAM 2003

As the years passed, Mel took a small step back from farm work and began to raise the next generation of Volantes: Dave, Teri, and Steve. Dave was born in 1981, with Teri and Steve following in 1985 and 1988, respectively. In between naps, baseball games, and Girl Scout meetings, Mel somehow found time for the mountains of bookwork piling up in the home office.

During this time, Al relied on the crew as much as ever to keep the farm going. Molly Lyne, Liz Bryden, Shu Chen, and Martin Dzengeleski kept the farm in order for decades. Others from this era are still doing so. Lynne Flodin came on to manage the farmstand and greenhouses in 1988. Her brother Lee joined a few years later to help Martin in the fields. Kerry Bez followed her daughters' footsteps into the farmstand, and Ryan Conroy joined in late 1996. Other familiar faces such as Dianne Porcello, Linda Mauro, and Mike McDermott all learned and perfected the Volante method of farming under Al and Ferdinand's watchful eyes. Growing up on the farm, Dave, Teri,

and Steve were able to watch Al and his crew work like a well-oiled machine, witnessing daily what hard work and loyalty could produce.

Today, Dave, Teri, and Steve have assumed their roles as the faces of the current generation at Volante Farms. Dave started working in the fields when he was very young; Al used to strap wooden blocks to the pedals of the cultivating tractor so Dave could reach them. In high school, Dave took over irrigation duties during the summers. When it was time to go off to college, he went around the corner to Babson, just like his father. Unlike his father, however, Dave wasn't carrying the fate of the farm on his shoulders while balancing his schoolwork. He graduated in 2003 and began to learn the ropes of running the business, which had settled comfortably into its traditions by this point.

The farm was humming along, but in true Volante spirit, there was always room for improvement. Anxious to make an impact and find opportunities to increase efficiency, Dave spearheaded the campaign to revamp the greenhouses. During the summer of 2007, the range of Al and Mel's hoop houses were razed. A state-of-the-art greenhouse rose in their place and opened in the spring of 2008. Dave installed a system that captured rainfall from the roof to use for irrigation, and as a result, water waste was soon at an all-time low. Radiant floors heated by high-efficiency natural gas boilers concentrated warmth at the plants' roots and made the workspace cozier in the winter months. Heat and shade curtains contributed to an ideal growing environment. The new greenhouse showcased an expanded selection of native and non-native plants and thus enhanced the experience for customers and staff.

Teri finished her studies at the University of Connecticut in 2007 and came to work full-time at the farm upon graduation. During that summer, she was tasked with making sure the farmstand ran smoothly while Dave was involved with the new greenhouse construction. She dove into the business, putting her skills to immediate use. Whether she was bunching cut flowers or joining forces with Mel and Kerry Bez to design the annual Trim-A-Tree shop, Teri's creative prowess became evident all around the farm.

Teri, like Mel before her, took on the role of welcoming the community to the family farm. She began outreach programs such as farm tours for local students and expanded the events schedule beyond the Corn Boil and Apple Pie Baking Contest to include a summer concert series and fundraisers for local food pantries. Working closely with Al, Teri assumed the farm's marketing operations. She continued to build strong relationships with local growers who have proven to be valuable partners for Volante Farms over the years. With the opening of the new farmstand, she has formed new bonds with countless artisanal grocers and local food purveyors.

Steve spent much of his early farm years pulling and cleaning scallions and helping to harvest lettuce and tomatoes. In 2010, fresh out of Boston College, he started working at the farm full-time and wedged himself into an increasingly crowded office. He helped with anything that needed to be done, from unloading deliveries in the greenhouse to taking on much of the irrigation duties during the summer. Now that Al's three children were involved, it was clear that the farm needed to grow as well. Steve took on many

Teri, Mel, Al, Steve, and Dave celebrating the first month in the new greenhouse, 2008.

of the technical aspects of the farmstand expansion plans, like integrating a new point-of-sale system and developing the new full-service kitchen, deli, and ice cream departments. Additionally, he worked to find season-extending crops for the new year-round business, heading up the planting of the asparagus crop at the Greenway field. In 2011, after more than two years of careful planning, construction began on the current farmstand. Just like in 1981, the farmstand's operations moved to the greenhouse during construction.

THE NEW FARMSTAND 2012

Al and Mel were now faced with one thing they had previously dreaded: year-round business. The new building was nearly five times the size of the previous stand, built with monstrous New England hemlock beams and sheathed in the same style of board and batten siding as the structure it was replacing.

Dave, Teri, and Steve split up responsibilities to embark on the new path of the family farm. Dave ran the overall farm and field operations; Teri oversaw the farmstand and retail components; and Steve handled all the new departments: kitchen, deli, bakery, and ice cream stand, to name a few. All three needed to beat a quick learning curve while tasked with managing a rapidly expanding staff.

Since opening in March of 2012, the new farmstand has aimed to provide a uniquely local resource for the community. The full-service deli builds fresh, top-quality sandwiches with homemade and homegrown toppings. The kitchen creates wholesome dishes using the expanded seasonal bounty of produce. The

Clockwise from top left: New greenhouse construction, summer 2007; Dave and Dianne Porcello carving pumpkins for charity, 2006; geraniums filling the greenhouse, 2009; another beautiful Christmas season, 2009.

ice cream stand features locally made frozen delights in the summer and harkens back to matriarch Caterina Volante's family ice cream business in Scotland. The beer and wine shop features a vast landscape of local beverages from upstart craft brewers, old cider houses, and fledgling vineyards.

When area butcher and longtime customer John Dewar closed his eponymous butcher shops in Newton and Wellesley, he approached the Volantes about a partnership. With his help, the Volantes brought his loyal customers and high-quality meats to the farmstand. Dewar wasn't the only venerable local purveyor to retire. After the Christmas of 2015, the farm's Central Avenue neighbor, Owen's Poultry Farm, shuttered its doors. This marked the loss of another multigenerational farm in Needham, leaving the Volantes with the only farmland in town under continuous cultivation since pre-colonial times.

Today's Volante Farms would be unrecognizable to Peter and Caterina. The fields still bring forth mountains of produce, but the seasons run longer. The farm's deli has become a breakfast and lunch hotspot, a meeting place for families on the go. Events include the long-running Apple Pie Baking Contest, cooking classes led by Chef Todd, gardening workshops in the spring, hands-on design projects, and multiple charity fundraisers intended to bring the community together. Now instead of the Volantes driving produce to the Boston market, the city travels to the farm for hanging baskets, heirloom tomatoes, hand-decorated Christmas wreaths, or a gourmet Dinner in the Field surrounded by the beautiful land in the former "sticks" of Needham.

NEEDHAM 2016

Dave, Teri, and Steve have all started families of their own, respectively bringing Katie, Stephen, and Erin into the family business. Dave's wife Katie took a particular interest in the business and, armed with two Babson degrees of her own, learned how to manage the farm's books under the supportive tutelage of Mel. Now that Mel is semi-retired, Katie meticulously handles the finances.

As of Volante Farms' hundredth anniversary, the fifth generation is represented by Ryan, William, Henry, and a couple goofy dogs. It will be just a few years before the kids are taught to drive tractors, scoop ice cream, harvest corn, water seedlings, and stack sandwiches. One thing is for sure: as these children grow, the farm will continue to adapt to provide for the community for generations to come.

WINTER

IN DECEMBER, when the fields are quieter, winter oats are spread as a cover crop on the tilled soil, forming a green carpet for piles of Christmas trees. The greenhouse is flush with evergreen boughs, hand-decorated wreaths, and vibrant poinsettias while glittering lights and ornaments twinkle. The most ardent customers roll in at eight o'clock the morning after Thanksgiving to pick out their family Christmas tree.

After the holiday rush, the farmstand quiets down. The relaxed pace of winter gives the staff the opportunity to repair, paint, and clean greenhouses and equipment. The field crew starts to pore over seed catalogs and plot out the next season's crop plan. In late January, we ready trays of soil for future transplants. The greenhouse warms up again in the first week of February, quickly filling with the earliest seedlings and hanging pots for the coming spring. Though brief, the short winter months are an opportune time to catch our breath, reflect on the past season, and start preparing for the year to come.

Sweet Beet Chips, page 258.

Winter Recipes

LEEK *and* PARSNIP SOUP

HARVEST VEGETABLE SOUP

GOLDEN BEET CHUTNEY

PICKLED RED ONIONS

CARAMELIZED ONION MARMALADE

·

SPICED WINTER CARROT SOUP

GARAM MASALA

PICKLED WINTER SQUASH

GRILLED CHEESE *with* BEER MUSTARD

ROASTED BRASSICAS *with* DIJON DRESSING

WINTER SQUASH GRATIN *with* CHESTNUTS

COLCANNON

ÜBER MASH

·

RAISIN SPAGHETTI

MAPLE BRINED PORK CHOPS *with* COLLARDS

BRAISED CHICKEN LEGS *with* WINTER VEGETABLES

NEW ENGLAND VEGETABLE "POT PIE"

·

STICKY TOFFEE PUDDING CAKE

FLOURLESS ALMOND CAKE

LEMON ALMOND TORTA

CHOCOLATE ESPRESSO TORTE

RED BEET VELVET CAKE

SWEET BEET CHIPS

EGGNOG CINNAMON CHIP SCONES

·

WINTER BEET OLD FASHIONED

PARSNIPS

WE have only been growing parsnips for a short while, but they have quickly become indispensable. We seed this amazing, season-extending vegetable in May. While the thick, white roots resemble carrots, they are much harder to harvest. One needs to apply a heavy boot to the pitchfork to loosen the soil. During some seasons, we go through several pitchforks; these roots go deep and one season's crop can outlast even the strongest tools.

Parsnips mature in late August and continue to improve in flavor through the fall. We harvest them until Thanksgiving as long as the ground hasn't frozen solid. Around Thanksgiving, we pull up enough to get through the holidays and mulch the remainder of the crop with hay to wait out the winter. In the spring, we pull off the hay and find the remaining parsnips pushing up little green leaves again. These parsnips are often the first fresh, homegrown flavor of the season and are met with applause despite their muddy, scarred appearance.

LEEK *and* PARSNIP SOUP

Leeks are among the farm's more regal-looking vegetables, and they are also somewhat misunderstood. Recipes usually only use the white lower quarter of the plant, typically discarding the fibrous upper green section, which is too tough to roast or cook into soups. When chopping leeks for this recipe, save the greens and use them in homemade stocks or thinly slice and fry them for a unique garnish.

This soup is healthy and delicious on its own but can be finished with a bit of cream or a dollop of crème fraîche for a richer approach.

SERVES 4 TO 6

4 tablespoons salted butter

4 parsnips (about 1 pound), peeled and cut into 1-inch pieces

2 tablespoons chopped garlic

2 large leeks (about 1 pound), white parts only, roughly chopped

2 medium Idaho potatoes (about 1 pound), peeled and cut into 2-inch pieces

10 sprigs thyme, tied with butcher's twine

Kosher salt, to taste

Black pepper, to taste

Melt butter in a soup pot over medium-high heat. Add parsnips and cook until they start to brown, about 10 to 12 minutes (stir sparingly to prevent sticking).

Add garlic, leeks, potatoes, thyme bundle, and a pinch of salt and pepper. Cook until leeks soften, about 8 to 10 minutes. Add enough water to just cover the vegetables, bring to a boil, and then lower to a simmer.

Cook until all vegetables are tender, about 25 to 30 minutes. Remove thyme bundle and squeeze any retained liquid into the soup.

Purée soup in the pot with an immersion blender. If you don't have an immersion blender, purée in small batches in a traditional blender and return the soup to the pot.

This soup will keep in the refrigerator for 5 days and in the freezer for up to 6 months.

HARVEST VEGETABLE SOUP

This is our staple cold-weather soup at the farm. We use several kinds of root vegetables to achieve its delicious, complex flavor. The cooking time varies for each of these vegetables, so you may need to use a few sheet pans to roast them all accordingly.

SERVES 4 TO 6

½ rutabaga (about ½ pound), peeled

½ celery root (about ½ pound), peeled

2 parsnips (about ½ pound), peeled

2 carrots (about ½ pound), peeled

½ butternut squash (about 1 pound), peeled, halved, and deseeded

6 tablespoons salted butter, melted, divided

Kosher salt, to taste

Black pepper, to taste

1 yellow onion, roughly chopped

1 tablespoon chopped garlic

Pinch of ground nutmeg

1 tablespoon chopped sage

Preheat oven to 400°F.

Cut rutabaga, celery root, parsnips, carrots, and squash into 1-inch cubes.

Keeping the vegetables separate, lightly coat each with 1 tablespoon butter and a pinch of salt and pepper.

Spread the rutabaga onto a sheet pan and roast in the oven for 10 minutes.

Add parsnips to the sheet pan, keeping vegetables in a single layer, and return the pan to the oven. Roast another 5 minutes, then add the carrots to the sheet pan, keeping all the vegetables in a single layer. (Use an additional sheet pan if necessary.) Return pan(s) to the oven and roast another 5 minutes.

Add the celery root and the squash and cook until all vegetables are tender, about another 30 minutes. (Total roasting time should be about 60 to 75 minutes.)

Place the remaining 1 tablespoon butter in a soup pot over medium heat, add onions, and cook until golden brown, about 12 to 14 minutes. Add garlic and cook for 3 minutes more.

Add roasted root vegetables and nutmeg to soup pot and enough water to just cover the vegetables. (Start with just this much, adding more water as necessary to thin the soup.)

Bring soup to a boil and then immediately lower heat to a simmer. Cook until all vegetables are soft, about 25 to 30 minutes.

Purée soup in the pot with an immersion blender or in small batches in a traditional blender.

Add sage and season to taste with salt and pepper. Serve warm.

This soup will keep in the refrigerator for 5 days and in the freezer for up to 6 months.

ALLIUMS

ALLIUMS—scallions, onions, garlic, and leeks—are such an everyday sight on the dinner table that it is easy to take them for granted. In reality, these crops take planning, patience, and attention while they form their precious bulbs.

Scallions are actually quite basic. These white, young onions go from seed to harvest in only a few months, ready to be incorporated into all sorts of dishes. We start these by planting small bulbs in early spring, followed by successive seedings throughout the summer.

Onions, which are more complicated, are seeded in the greenhouse in January. In May, we dig individual holes five inches apart in a raised bed where we transplant the ten thousand or so onion seedlings. They are ready for harvest in mid-July and sold with their greens intact. Eventually the remaining onions are harvested to dry and cure in the barn for long-term storage and fall sales.

Leeks are even more particular. They are seeded right after the onions and are also planted in May. Unlike onions, however, we plant the leeks single-file so we can eventually straddle them with a cultivating tractor. We open a hole with a stick or trowel handle, drop in the root, and walk away. We prefer to time this planting around an impending rain so the drops will gently fill in the holes to settle the leeks in place without suffocating the growing tips. We mound soil around them as they continue to grow taller over the next seven months so that they will form clean, white bulbs with flavor-packed, pale green centers. We will harvest these vegetables right into the winter whenever the ground is not frozen.

The crop that best exemplifies the concept of delayed gratification is garlic. We break up garlic cloves and push them into the earth in October, before the ground freezes. Green spikes usually pop up shortly before winter, which we mulch with straw. Come spring, the garlic shoots send out a fan of flagging leaves. Eventually, in late May, a flower stalk starts to emerge from the center. This scape curls out of the bulb in an attempt to mature and fling seeds far from its home. We pluck the scapes early, however, after just a few twists and turns, allowing the sun's rays to concentrate on bulking up the head of garlic in the ground. In recent years, the wild-looking pale green scapes have caught the eye of customers who prize them for their mild garlicky flavor and as an early sign of spring.

The garlic patch takes about a month to fully scape. By that time, we have started pulling fresh stalks with bulbous bottoms. This fresh garlic is the result of a nine-month commitment, and that's before we pull the bulbs we dry and cure for storage. Garlic represents every farmer's optimism, as it requires investment in the next year's season before winter even arrives.

BEETS

BEETS are a particular crop for particular tastes. We grow them spring, summer, and fall and consider them an excellent winter vegetable because they store so well. We seed our first beets of the season alongside the peas in early spring. We harvest the first young beets just for their greens, allowing us to thin the rows. Beet greens are great to toss into salads or to sauté, like spinach. Their bitter taste belies the sweet roots forming underneath. Deep burgundy reds, the candy cane stripe of the Chioggia, and bright golden beets all provide a hit of sugar and earthy flavor.

GOLDEN BEET CHUTNEY

We are always amazed at how versatile beets are—and this chutney proves the point. Serve this alongside chicken or pork, or even on a salad.

MAKES 1 TO 2 CUPS

3 to 4 golden beets (about 1 pound), rinsed and greens removed

2 tablespoons olive oil

½ teaspoon whole mustard seed

½ teaspoon whole cumin seed

2 tablespoons minced ginger

½ cup cider vinegar

2 tablespoons granulated sugar

3 tablespoons golden raisins

Pinch of red pepper flakes

Kosher salt, to taste

Pinch of paprika

⅓ cup Pickled Red Onions, diced (pg. 222)

1 teaspoon chopped cilantro

Peel beets and cut into a small dice.

Heat olive oil in a large sauté pan over medium heat. Add mustard and cumin seeds and cook for 20 seconds. Add beets and cook for 2 minutes. Add ginger and cook another 2 minutes.

Add vinegar and reduce by half, about 8 to 10 minutes.

Add sugar, raisins, red pepper flakes, and a pinch of salt and paprika and cook until beets are tender, about 18 to 20 minutes.

Remove from heat and let cool. Fold in Pickled Red Onions and cilantro. Season to taste with additional salt if needed.

This chutney will keep in the refrigerator for 2 weeks.

PICKLED RED ONIONS

2 red onions (about 1 pound), thinly sliced

1 cup cider vinegar

1½ cups water

1½ teaspoons granulated sugar

2 teaspoons kosher salt

1 tablespoon pickling spice

Place onions in a bowl and set aside.

Bring remaining ingredients to a boil in a pot. Immediately remove from heat and let cool for 10 minutes.

Strain liquid over onions. Discard the pickling spice. Let onions cool and store in the refrigerator for up to 2 weeks.

Use these onions on everything!

CARAMELIZED ONION MARMALADE

This marmalade is exceptionally versatile. We use it on everything from sandwiches to pasta, and it makes an especially great addition to pork dishes. If you don't have any cider syrup kicking around, you can substitute apple cider in a pinch—just double the amount.

3 tablespoons olive oil

3 medium red onions (about 1½ pounds), thinly sliced

1 tablespoon chopped garlic

1 tablespoon cider vinegar

3 tablespoons cider syrup (or ¼ cup apple cider)

Kosher salt, to taste

Black pepper, to taste

1 teaspoon chopped thyme

Heat olive oil in a large sauté pan or a wide-bottomed pot over medium-high heat.

Add onions and resist the temptation to stir them for the first 8 to 10 minutes. (Stirring will cause them to release moisture, making it harder for them to brown.)

Once the onions start to color, stir and continue cooking until they achieve a deep golden brown, about 25 to 35 minutes more, adjusting the heat as necessary to prevent them from burning.

Add garlic and cook for 2 minutes. Add vinegar and cook for 1 minute. Add syrup and a pinch of salt and pepper and cook for about 3 minutes. (If using cider, cook until almost no liquid remains, about 8 minutes.) The goal is a jelly-like consistency.

Remove from heat, fold in chopped thyme, and let cool.

Season to taste with salt and pepper.

This marmalade will keep in the refrigerator for 1 week.

Crostini three ways: Caramelized Onion Marmalade;
Golden Beet Chutney, pg. 221; Arugula Pesto, pg. 104
with Pickled Winter Squash, pg. 228.

SPICED WINTER CARROT SOUP

SERVES 4 TO 6

½ cup olive oil, divided

4 to 6 medium carrots (about 1½ pounds), peeled and roughly chopped

Kosher salt, to taste

1 medium yellow onion, roughly chopped

2 sweet potatoes (about 1 pound), peeled and roughly chopped

1 tablespoon chopped garlic

1½ tablespoons chopped ginger

½ tablespoon Garam Masala (pg. 227)

1½ quarts chicken or vegetable stock

1 tablespoon pomegranate molasses

1 cup coconut milk, divided

1 tablespoon cilantro

Seeds from 1 pomegranate

Heat ¼ cup olive oil in a soup pot over medium-high heat. Add carrots and a pinch of salt and cook until golden brown, about 10 to 12 minutes. Remove from pot and set aside.

Add remaining olive oil to pot with onions, sweet potatoes, and another pinch of salt. Cook until onions begin to brown, about 10 to 12 minutes.

Add garlic and ginger and cook for 5 minutes, stirring occasionally. Sprinkle in Garam Masala and cook for 1 minute.

Pour enough stock over vegetables until they are just covered, adding more if necessary. Bring to a boil and then immediately reduce heat to a simmer. Stir occasionally, cooking until the vegetables become tender, about 30 to 40 minutes.

Remove from heat, stir in pomegranate molasses and coconut milk, reserving 1 tablespoon for garnish, and season to taste with salt.

Purée soup in the pot with an immersion blender. If you don't have an immersion blender, purée in small batches in a traditional blender and ladle into bowls.

Garnish with swirl of reserved coconut milk, chopped cilantro, and pomegranate seeds and serve warm.

This soup, without garnish, will keep in the refrigerator for 5 days and in the freezer for up to 6 months.

GARAM MASALA

We make our own garam masala (a ground Indian spice mixture) in house. Any store-bought mix will work well, but the vibrancy of a freshly roasted and ground mix goes a long way. We use this spice blend in a number of recipes, including our Spiced Winter Carrot Soup. Cooking the vegetables with the dry spice mixture right before adding stock releases a tremendous aroma and deepens the flavor of the finished soup.

MAKES ABOUT ½ CUP

2 tablespoons whole
cardamom seed

1 teaspoon whole cloves

2½ teaspoons whole black
peppercorns

1 teaspoon whole fennel seed

2 tablespoons whole
coriander seed

5 teaspoons whole cumin seed

¾ teaspoon whole mustard
seed

Pinch of ground cinnamon

Pinch of ground fenugreek

Pinch of ground nutmeg

Pinch of ground turmeric

Heat cardamom seed in a dry sauté pan over lowest heat possible on stove. After 2 minutes, add cloves.

Every 2 minutes add the next ingredient on the list, ending with the mustard seed. Remove pan from heat and add remaining spices. Let cool.

Place cooled mixture into a spice grinder and pulse into a powder.

The sooner you use it the better, but this spice will keep in a sealed container for up to 4 months.

PICKLED WINTER SQUASH

Here's a twist on a tried-and-true technique. Pickled winter squash is a surefire way to add a kick of color to any winter day. This recipe is full of flavor and suits a variety of root vegetables. Try substituting parsnips, carrots, or sweet potatoes—heck, you could do a mixture of them all!

MAKES ABOUT 4 CUPS

1 winter squash (about 1 pound), peeled and deseeded

1¼ cups rice vinegar

1½ cups water

3 tablespoons granulated sugar

2 tablespoons kosher salt

1½ teaspoons crystalized ginger

2 pieces star anise

1 tablespoon whole black peppercorns

½ teaspoon pickling spice

2 fresh bay leaves

Slice squash as thinly as possible and place in a bowl.

Add all remaining ingredients to a pot and bring to a boil. Immediately remove from heat and let cool for 10 minutes. Pour liquid over squash and let sit until cool.

Transfer squash and liquid to a container and seal tightly. Let sit in the refrigerator for one week before using.

Add the squash to slaws, mix it into salads, and stack it on sandwiches. This squash will keep in the refrigerator for up to 6 months.

GRILLED CHEESE *with* BEER MUSTARD

Some recipes are carefully thought out ahead of time. But not this one. This sandwich was born during the first cold winter in the new farmstand to satisfy a simple craving. Recipes are great, but sometimes you just have to follow your stomach.

MAKES 1 SANDWICH

3 slices bacon (we like our house-made Volante Farms bacon)

2 tablespoons Beer Mustard

2 slices good, crusty sandwich bread

6 slices sharp cheddar

2 tablespoons salted butter, divided

1 apple (we like Honeycrisp, Pinova, or Ginger Gold), thinly sliced

Arrange bacon slices in a cold skillet. Cook over medium-low heat to your liking. When bacon is done, set aside and drain on paper towels. Reserve bacon fat in pan.

Lightly spread Beer Mustard on both pieces of bread. Add cheese and bacon.

Melt butter in the same pan over medium heat and place bread into hot butter, cheese sides up. Cook until golden brown. Remove from pan and layer sliced apples on one half.

Put sandwich together and enjoy!

BEER MUSTARD

We love our winter squash for their versatility and flavor, but with all the fall harvest choices available they aren't exactly the belles of the ball. Shiny apples and warm cider donuts are stiff competition come October, and we always end up with more squash than we know what to do with after the Thanksgiving rush.

Luckily for us, we made friends with a couple brewers down the road who love our squash almost as much as we do. Jack's Abby Brewing, a rapidly growing family business about nine miles away in Framingham, makes their fantastic Pumpkin Crop Lager using the season's pumpkins and all that delicious winter squash.

The resulting beer is full of fall flavor, is the perfect backbone for this mustard, and allows us to sneak our homegrown produce into a winter recipe. This recipe yields a good amount, so jar some up for your favorite foodie.

MAKES 4 CUPS

1½ cups Jack's Abby Pumpkin Crop Lager

1 cup cider vinegar

½ cup malt vinegar

⅓ cup honey

¼ cup brown sugar

½ cup yellow mustard seed

½ cup brown mustard seed

2 teaspoons kosher salt

1 teaspoon ground cloves

1 teaspoon ground allspice

1 cup apple cider

⅔ teaspoon ground turmeric

1 cup ground mustard

Simmer beer in a pot for 10 minutes. Add both vinegars and simmer for 5 minutes. Stir in honey, brown sugar, both mustard seeds, salt, cloves, and allspice. Remove from heat and allow to sit overnight.

The next day, combine the seedy beer mixture with the cider, turmeric, and ground mustard. Using an immersion blender or working in batches with a conventional blender, grind the mixture so that it's only slightly combined. The majority of the seeds should stay intact.

If the mixture is too thick, add cider to thin it out.

This mustard will keep in a sealed container in the refrigerator for 2 to 3 months.

CARROTS

CARROTS are probably the closest thing we have to a year-round crop in New England. We seed them in early March and begin to harvest them in June, with several successive plantings following through the summer. We usually grow them at the Standish farm, as the home field is too rocky for forking and carrots from the Greenway fields often taste bitter.

Using a pitchfork to loosen the soil around the roots, we pop the carrots out and inspect them. For many decades, we sold the carrots bunched with their greens. Every cash register was equipped with a produce knife to remove the greens for customers without rabbits at home to feed. Recently, however, we discovered customers love being able to choose just how many carrots they want. So now we sell them loose without greens throughout the year.

After pulling fresh carrots from the field, we rely on the storage capabilities of our new farmstand. Right before the Christmas season we yank as many as we can from the last crop and pile them under wet burlap in large wooden bins, where they will live in a dark, cool corner of the farmstand for the winter. We will even mulch what remains in the field in the hopes they will survive the winter (and hungry deer) and we can pull them in the spring. This usually happens about the same time we are seeding the next year's crop, so the gap without carrots is the briefest of any of our homegrown vegetables.

Field Manager Ryan Conroy has planted the farm's carrots since taking over for Marty in 2000.

ROASTED BRASSICAS *with* DIJON DRESSING

1 small head broccoli

1 small head romanesco

1 red bell pepper, cut into strips

1½ cups olive oil, divided

Kosher salt, to taste

Black pepper, to taste

½ pound brussels sprouts, trimmed and halved

¼ cup white wine vinegar

2 tablespoons lemon juice

½ teaspoon anchovy paste

1 teaspoon chopped capers

1 teaspoon Dijon mustard

Preheat oven to 425°F.

Cut broccoli and romanesco into florets by placing their heads face up on a cutting board. Quarter the heads to create smaller, more manageable wedges. Slice the florets off the exposed stalks, discarding the stalks when finished.

Lightly coat the bell pepper with 1 tablespoon olive oil and a pinch of salt and pepper. Roast on a sheet pan for 12 to 15 minutes, then set aside. While the bell pepper is cooking, place 2 empty sheet pans in the oven to preheat for the next step.

Keeping the vegetables separate, lightly coat the romanesco and broccoli with 4 tablespoons olive oil each and a pinch of both salt and pepper. Lightly coat the brussels sprouts with 2 tablespoons olive oil and a pinch of salt and pepper.

Remove preheated pans from the oven and place the vegetables on the pans (or pieces of foil if they are sharing pans). Roast the vegetables until tender, about 15 to 20 minutes for broccoli and 20 to 25 minutes for romanesco and brussels sprouts.

While vegetables are roasting, combine white wine vinegar, lemon juice, anchovy paste, capers, mustard, and a pinch of salt and pepper in a bowl. Slowly add remaining olive oil (about ¾ cup), whisking constantly, to create dressing. Season to taste with additional salt and pepper.

Once brassicas are cooked, combine them, add roasted pepper, lightly coat with dressing, and season to taste once more if needed.

Serve warm on its own as a side dish or on a bed of lettuce for a hearty salad.

VOLANTE FARMS

234

WINTER SQUASH

BETTER suited to farms with more land than ours, winter squashes—like pumpkins and buttercups—spread across the odd corners of our fields toward the end of the spring planting season. Requiring less care after planting than other vegetables, the dozen or so varieties we grow stretch and tumble over each other for months. The squash crop is inevitably a weedy mess come fall because, during the summer, we try to avoid tromping around on the network of vines and let the invading weeds battle with the hubbard and acorn squashes for acreage. While it is far from Dave's favorite crop, the field crew looks forward to the squash pick every year. The harvest commences in September when the colorful orbs litter the field. We cut their stems and toss them like medicine balls from one person to the next, moving the squash down the rows toward the truck. From there, we fling them to the crewmembers perched between the large waiting cardboard bins. We do not have enough land here in the suburbs to grow all the pumpkins we need to satisfy the Halloween demand, so we trust growers like Araujo Farms in Dighton to truck in ton after ton of the orange globes and their more edible cousins each October. From Wee-Bee Littles to Atlantic Giants, our pumpkins range in size from baseball to boat. As fall sets in and corn wanes, winter squash and pumpkins take over nooks in the barn, farmstand, and greenhouse, where they cure and wait to become part of a meal or other holiday tableau.

WINTER SQUASH GRATIN *with* CHESTNUTS

SERVES 4 TO 6 AS A SIDE

1 winter squash (about 2 to 2½ pounds)

8 tablespoons salted butter, melted, divided

Kosher salt, to taste

Black pepper, to taste

1 large yellow onion, thinly sliced

1 tablespoon chopped sage, divided

1½ cups plain breadcrumbs

½ cup cooked chestnuts, chopped

1½ tablespoons brown sugar

1 teaspoon ground cinnamon

Preheat oven to 425°F.

Cut squash in half and discard seeds, leaving the skin intact. Place on a sheet pan cut side up. Drizzle with 2 tablespoons melted butter and sprinkle with salt and pepper. Roast until golden brown and tender, about 35 to 45 minutes.

Meanwhile, add 2 tablespoons butter to a large sauté pan over medium heat. Add onions and a pinch of salt and pepper, stirring together to coat. Cook untouched until onions start to brown, about 8 to 10 minutes, then stir and reduce heat slightly. Continue to cook, stirring occasionally, until onions are an even, dark brown, about 25 to 30 minutes total. Add ½ tablespoon of sage to the onions, remove from heat, and set aside.

Mix together breadcrumbs, chestnuts, 3 tablespoons melted butter, and a pinch of salt and pepper.

When the squash is cooked, remove from oven and let cool. Scoop flesh into a bowl and add remaining butter, the remaining sage, brown sugar, and cinnamon. Mash well. Mix in onions and season to taste with salt and pepper.

Reduce oven temperature to 375°F.

Scoop squash mixture into a 9-by-13-inch baking dish and cover with breadcrumb mixture. Bake until top is golden brown, about 12 to 15 minutes. Remove from oven and serve warm.

COLCANNON

SERVES 4 TO 6 AS A SIDE

2 to 3 medium Idaho potatoes (about 1½ pounds), peeled and quartered

Kosher salt, to taste

8 tablespoons salted butter, divided

1 medium yellow onion, thinly sliced

1 tablespoon chopped garlic

½ head green cabbage (about 1 pound), thinly sliced

Black pepper, to taste

1 cup light cream

1 tablespoon chopped parsley

Place potatoes and a pinch of salt in a pot with enough water to just cover the potatoes. Bring to a boil and then immediately reduce heat to simmer. Simmer until the potatoes are tender, about 20 to 30 minutes. Strain, reserve 1 cup cooking liquid, and place potatoes in a large mixing bowl.

Meanwhile, heat 2 tablespoons of butter in a large sauté pan over medium heat. Add onions and cook until deep golden brown, 12 to 15 minutes. Add garlic and cook for 3 minutes. Add cabbage and a pinch of salt and pepper and cook for 10 minutes. Pour reserved cup of cooking liquid into pan and cook until cabbage is tender, about 5 minutes.

In a small saucepot, heat cream and the remaining butter over medium heat until combined. Mash potatoes while slowly adding the cream/butter mixture. Fold cabbage mixture into potatoes, sprinkle with parsley, and season to taste with salt and pepper.

Serve warm in lieu of mashed potatoes.

ÜBER MASH

Here's a twist on standard mashed potatoes. This dish is great around the holidays with roasted turkey and cranberry chutney.

SERVES 4 TO 6 AS A SIDE

3 baking potatoes (about 1½ pounds)

2 parsnips (about ½ pound)

½ celery root (about ½ pound)

1 teaspoon kosher salt, plus more to taste

3 tablespoons salted butter, at room temperature

½ cup sour cream

1 teaspoon freshly grated horseradish

Black pepper, to taste

1 tablespoon chopped chives

Peel and halve the potatoes and peel and cut the parsnips and celery root into 1-inch pieces. Combine potatoes, parsnips, and celery root in a large pot of water and add 1 teaspoon salt.

Bring to a boil and then reduce heat to simmer. Cook until tender, about 20 to 30 minutes. Drain well, transfer to a large bowl, and mash vegetables.

Add butter, sour cream, horseradish, and a pinch of salt and pepper to the vegetables.

Mash until well incorporated. Mix in the chives and season to taste with salt and pepper.

Serve hot.

RAISIN SPAGHETTI

Not only is this pasta dish delicious, it's authentic, too. You can find similar recipes under the name "Spaghetti Corleonese," originating from the town of Corleone (yes, that Corleone), which is in Sicily. While most recipes add pine nuts, walnuts, and a whole mess of other ingredients to the mix, we were raised on a simpler preparation. In the Volante household, this seemingly bizarre dish is served alongside a host of varied seafood dishes every year on Christmas Eve as part of the Feast of the Seven Fishes, an Italian-American tradition.

Ferdinand made it throughout our entire childhood. Since his passing, family friend Elio Angelucci has taken the reins, preparing the anchovy-laden oil for us around the holidays. Driving to pick it up at his home in Dover at ten o'clock in the morning is almost as fun as the meal itself, since Elio—in true Italian-American fashion—makes wine and grappa in his well-stocked cellar. The morning sampling of various oak-barreled treats typically leads to a "riposo" in the afternoon (translation: wine nap).

– Steve Volante

SERVES 4 TO 6

1 pound spaghetti

¾ cup olive oil

4 ounces anchovies

3 tablespoons chopped garlic

⅔ cup raisins

Kosher salt, to taste

Black pepper, to taste

Freshly grated Asiago cheese, for garnish (optional)

Chopped parsley, for garnish (optional)

Prepare pasta according to package instructions, stopping just shy of al dente.

While pasta is cooking, add olive oil to a large skillet over medium-low heat. Add anchovies and sauté for about 10 to 15 minutes, breaking up the anchovies into a paste.

Add garlic to pan and brown for 2 to 3 minutes, stirring. Add raisins to the pan and cook for 2 minutes. Season to taste with salt and pepper. (Careful with the salt here. The anchovies add a good amount of saltiness to this dish, but seasoning the sauce to bring out the flavors is still necessary.)

Add pasta to the skillet, stir, and simmer for two minutes more, thoroughly coating it with the sauce. Garnish with parsley or cheese if desired.

MAPLE BRINED PORK CHOPS *with* COLLARDS

Brining pork is a great way to ensure a delicious final product. The salt water bath allows the meat to absorb salt, moisture, and seasonings for a juicier and more dynamic dish. We use a little maple syrup for flavor in this recipe, but you can try bay leaves, peppercorns, or any other spices you like. Bring flavorful pork back to the table!

SERVES 4

BRINE

½ **gallon hot water**

½ **cup maple syrup**

½ **cup kosher salt**

4 **bone-in pork chops**

COLLARDS

3 **tablespoons olive oil, divided**

4 **slices bacon**

Black pepper, to taste

1 **large yellow onion, thinly sliced**

1 **tablespoon chopped garlic**

1 **cup apple cider**

1 **bunch collard greens (about 1 pound), stems discarded and roughly chopped**

Kosher salt, to taste

Make brine. Stir together water, maple syrup, and salt until fully dissolved and refrigerate until cool. Submerge pork chops in brine and refrigerate for at least 8 hours. If time allows, brine overnight. Remove pork chops from brine and pat dry.

Preheat a sheet pan in the oven to 375°F.

Heat 2 tablespoons olive oil in a wide-bottomed pot over medium-high heat. Add bacon and cook 6 to 8 minutes, until golden brown. Remove bacon from the pot and set aside.

Lightly sprinkle pork chops with pepper, then brown in the rendered bacon fat, about 4 to 5 minutes each side.

Once browned, place chops on preheated sheet pan. Roast chops until they reach an internal temperature of 145°F, about 15 to 18 minutes.

While the chops are roasting, heat the remaining 1 tablespoon olive oil in the same pot over medium-high heat and add the onions. Cook until golden brown, about 10 to 12 minutes. Add garlic and cook until brown, about 1 to 2 minutes.

Add apple cider and reduce to about ⅓ cup. Add collards and a pinch of salt and pepper. Reduce heat and cover, stirring occasionally. Cook until the leaves wilt, about 12 to 15 minutes, making sure they are al dente to the bite. Remove from heat and stir in bacon.

When the pork chops are cooked, remove from oven and let rest for 3 to 5 minutes.

Serve with collards and a hearty side. Über Mash (pg. 239), Winter Squash Biscuits (pg. 248), or Corn, Okra, and Bacon Fritters (pg. 160) make great companions for this dish.

BRAISED CHICKEN LEGS *with* WINTER VEGETABLES

SERVES 4

3 tablespoons olive oil

4 chicken legs

Kosher salt, to taste

Black pepper, to taste

1 rutabaga (about 1 pound),
peeled and diced

2 carrots (about ½ pound),
peeled and diced

2 medium yellow onions
(about 1 pound), chopped

2 tablespoons chopped garlic

4 cups chicken stock

4 cups water

½ pound assorted potatoes,
quartered

1 bunch chopped kale (about
4 cups)

2 tablespoons chopped thyme

Add olive oil to a large braising pan or dutch oven over medium-high heat.

Season chicken legs with salt and pepper, place carefully in pan, and cook until golden brown on both sides, about 4 to 5 minutes per side. Remove from pan and set aside.

Add rutabaga to pan and cook until golden brown, about 8 to 10 minutes, and set aside. Add carrots, lightly brown them, about 8 to 10 minutes, and set aside. Add onions and cook until golden brown, about 8 to 10 minutes. Add garlic to onions and cook for 1 minute. Add chicken stock and water and bring to boil.

Add chicken, rutabaga, and carrots, reduce heat, and simmer for 20 minutes. Add potatoes and cook for another 12 minutes. Add kale and simmer for an additional 10 minutes, all the while checking to make sure the rest of the vegetables are cooking evenly. Add thyme and season to taste with salt and pepper.

Divide vegetables into bowls, place chicken legs over vegetables, and ladle some of the braising liquid on top. Serve immediately.

NEW ENGLAND VEGETABLE "POT PIE"

This is serious comfort food. This vegetarian recipe is exceptionally hearty—perfect for a winter Sunday. The combination of rich gravy and root vegetables on top of buttery biscuits almost demands to be eaten on a couch while wrapped in a wool blanket. If the carnivores in your family put up a fuss, add cooked chicken or turkey to the mixture for something a little more traditional.

SERVES 4 TO 6

FILLING

2 carrots (about ½ pound), peeled

2 to 3 Yukon Gold potatoes (about 1 pound)

2 parsnips (about ½ pound), peeled

½ celery root (about ½ pound), peeled

8 tablespoons salted butter, divided

2 large leeks (about 1 pound), white parts only, diced

3 tablespoons chopped garlic

1 tablespoon chopped thyme

⅔ cup all-purpose flour

1¼ quarts vegetable stock, warmed

½ bunch chopped kale (about 2 cups)

Kosher salt, to taste

Black pepper, to taste

Preheat oven to 425°F.

Make filling. Cut carrots, potatoes, parsnips, and celery root into 1-inch cubes.

Heat 1 tablespoon butter in a large, wide-bottomed pot over medium-high heat. Add carrots and brown, about 8 to 10 minutes, then remove from pot and set aside. Repeat this step with potatoes, parsnips, and celery root, adding 1 tablespoon of butter per vegetable.

Lower heat to medium and add remaining butter to pot. Add leeks and cook for 6 to 8 minutes. Add garlic and thyme and cook for 3 minutes.

Slowly whisk in flour, stirring constantly to prevent burning. Cook until the mixture thickens to form a roux, about 4 to 5 minutes. Slowly whisk in stock until a thick sauce is formed. Simmer for another 5 minutes.

Remove from heat, combine with vegetables and kale, and season to taste with salt and pepper.

Pour mixture into a 9-by-13-inch baking dish. Place pot pie filling in oven and cook for 20 to 25 minutes until piping hot, then remove from oven and set aside.

WINTER SQUASH BISCUITS
MAKES 6 TO 8 BISCUITS

½ small winter squash (about 1 pound)

1 tablespoon olive oil

1 tablespoon kosher salt

½ teaspoon black pepper

2½ cups all-purpose flour

3 tablespoons brown sugar

1 tablespoon baking powder

½ teaspoon ground nutmeg

3 tablespoons shortening, cold

4 tablespoons salted butter, cubed, cold

2 tablespoons whole milk, plus more for brushing

1 tablespoon chopped sage

Make biscuits. Cut squash in half and discard seeds, leaving skin intact. Lightly coat squash with olive oil and a pinch of salt and pepper. Roast cut side down until golden brown, about 35 to 45 minutes, and remove from oven. When cool enough to handle, scrape out flesh and mash in a bowl, reserving 1 cup mashed squash. (A pound of uncooked squash will yield about 1½ cups cooked and mashed squash.) Discard remaining squash.

Mix flour, brown sugar, baking powder, salt, pepper, and nutmeg together in a large bowl. Add shortening and butter and gently mix together by hand.

Add squash, milk, and sage to bowl and mix thoroughly. Keep in mind that the squash can vary in moisture. Add more flour if the dough is too sticky.

Lightly flour a work surface and knead dough for 20 to 30 seconds; do not overwork the dough.

Roll the dough out until it is about ½- to 1-inch thick. Using a circular cutter, cut out biscuits and place them on sheet pan. Lightly brush biscuits with milk and bake until golden, about 12 to 14 minutes.

To serve, place a biscuit in the bottom of each bowl and ladle pot pie filling over top.

These biscuits can also be eaten warm with lots of butter and smothered in Rhubarb and Thyme Jam (pg. 40).

FARMING COMMUNITY

THE farming business in New England is so intertwined that it is often more important to learn from neighboring farms than it is to beat them in the marketplace. This means that small farms can work together to make sure each farmstand can provide a variety of local produce for its customers.

Ferdinand Volante was a smart farmer and savvy businessman. He worked to simultaneously establish connections within the Italian community and to sustain the connections his father-in-law, Peter, had made within the New England farming community. Many of these multigenerational farms have been working with the Volantes since the beginning, allowing the families to share advice and products.

A good example of this collaborative effort is our relationship with Mario Marini and his family in Ipswich. Their coastal location means a later frost and thus a longer lasting tomato crop, while Volantes' protected inland location might yield spring peas before Marini's.

Volante Farms has also partnered with the families at D&D Farms and Cavicchio Greenhouses in Sudbury for decades. Both of these farms were major produce suppliers in Ferdinand's day, though they have since transitioned into primarily ornamental plant growers.

Similarly, A. Russo & Sons has been doing business with the Volante family since the early days; a young Tony Russo was often seen riding on the back of delivery trucks at the Newton farm in the 1950s. Volante Farms still sources much of its non-homegrown produce from Russo's of Watertown.

Recently the Volantes have collaborated with Tougas Family Farm, a beautiful Northborough orchard that is taking familiar steps to pass the business from one generation to the next. This tradition of cooperation has been instrumental to Volante Farms' story.

STICKY TOFFEE PUDDING CAKE

MAKES ONE 9-INCH CAKE ─────────────────────────────

CAKE

½ pound dates, pitted

1¾ cups hot coffee

1 teaspoon baking soda

8 tablespoons salted butter, cubed, cold

¼ cup plus 2 tablespoons brown sugar

2 eggs

1 teaspoon vanilla extract

1½ cups all-purpose flour

¼ teaspoon iodized salt

1½ tablespoons baking powder

TOFFEE SAUCE

8 tablespoons butter, cold

½ cup brown sugar

¼ cup heavy cream

1 teaspoon vanilla extract

Pinch of iodized salt

Put dates and coffee in a saucepan and bring to a boil. Remove from heat and let cool, about 1 hour. Purée in a food processor until smooth, stir in baking soda, and set aside.

Preheat oven to 300°F.

Grease a 9-inch cake pan with butter or cooking spray. Line pan with a circle of parchment paper, then grease paper as well.

Using a hand mixer or stand mixer fitted with the paddle attachment, cream the butter and sugar on high until very light and fluffy, about 3 to 5 minutes.

Reduce speed to medium, add eggs and vanilla extract, and mix for 2 minutes. Scrape down sides of bowl and mix for an additional minute.

In a separate bowl, stir together flour, salt, and baking powder and set aside.

Reduce mixer speed to low. Slowly add some of the flour mixture, followed by some of the date and coffee mixture. Repeat process until mixtures are incorporated into a thick batter.

Pour batter into prepared cake pan and bake until the cake is dark brown and springs back slightly when touched, about 1 hour.

While the cake is baking, make the toffee sauce.

Combine all sauce ingredients in a small saucepan. Bring to a boil and then immediately reduce heat to simmer. Simmer and stir for about 2 minutes until sauce thickens and blends.

Remove cake from oven and poke all over the top with a toothpick or skewer so that sauce will seep into the cake. Pour ½ cup warm toffee sauce over the cake while it is still in pan. Let rest 15 minutes and then unmold cake onto serving platter.

Serve warm with extra toffee sauce drizzled on top or on the side. It's messy, but boy is it good.

FLOURLESS ALMOND CAKE

MAKES ONE 9-INCH CAKE ───────────────────────────────

8 ounces sliced almonds

½ teaspoon iodized salt

1¼ cups granulated sugar, divided

1 cup grated or finely chopped dark chocolate

6 eggs, separated

Zest of 1 orange

¼ teaspoon almond extract

8 to 12 orange slices, for garnish

Preheat oven to 350°F.

Finely grind almonds, salt, and ½ cup sugar in a food processor. Stir in chocolate and set aside.

In a large bowl, whip egg whites and ¼ cup sugar using a stand mixer or hand mixer on high until stiff peaks form, about 3 minutes, and set aside.

In a separate bowl, combine egg yolks, ½ cup sugar, orange zest, and almond extract. Whip on high for 3 minutes. (Make sure to whip egg whites first. If you whip yolks first, you will have to clean whisk before whipping egg whites.)

Stir whipped yolk mixture and almond mixture together, creating a thick, oatmeal-like batter. Fold in egg whites gently but thoroughly.

Grease a 9-inch spring-form pan with butter or cooking spray. Scoop batter into pan. Bake in oven until golden brown on top, about 45 to 50 minutes.

Garnish with orange slices and serve at room temperature with vanilla ice cream.

LEMON ALMOND TORTA

LEMON CURD

¾ cup granulated sugar

3 eggs

½ cup lemon juice

4 tablespoons lemon zest

Pinch of iodized salt

4 tablespoons salted butter, cubed, cold

CAKE

½ cup sliced almonds, plus more for topping

1 cup all-purpose flour

1 teaspoon baking powder

½ teaspoon iodized salt

8 tablespoons salted butter, cubed, cold

1 cup granulated sugar

1 teaspoon vanilla extract

1 teaspoon almond extract

3 eggs at room temperature, lightly beaten

Powdered sugar, for garnish

Make lemon curd. Whisk together sugar, eggs, lemon juice, zest, and salt in non-aluminum, heavy-bottomed saucepan.

Cook over medium heat, whisking constantly until thickened, about 5 to 10 minutes. Pour mixture into bowl, add butter, and stir until melted and fully incorporated. Gently press plastic wrap onto top of curd, covering completely (this prevents a skin from forming). Refrigerate at least 2 hours or overnight.

Once the lemon curd is ready, prepare the cake. Grease a 9-inch cake pan with butter or cooking spray. Line pan with a circle of parchment paper, then grease paper as well. Press a handful of sliced almonds onto the bottom and sides of the pan.

Preheat oven to 350°F. Grind almonds, flour, baking powder, and salt in a food processor and set aside.

Using a hand mixer or stand mixer fitted with the paddle attachment, cream butter and sugar on high until very light and fluffy, about 3 to 5 minutes.

Add vanilla and almond extracts to bowl and mix on medium speed for another minute to incorporate.

Add dry almond mixture and mix on low for an additional 1 to 2 minutes, scraping sides of bowl. With mixer running, add eggs and increase speed to medium. Mix until batter is thick.

Pour batter into pan and spread evenly. Spread lemon curd over batter, almost to the edges of the pan (but not touching). Sprinkle the top with a few sliced almonds. Bake for 30 minutes, then lower temperature to 325°F and continue baking until the top of the cake is golden, about 10 to 15 minutes.

Cool to room temperature (about 1 hour) before unmolding. Sprinkle with powdered sugar and enjoy!

CHOCOLATE ESPRESSO TORTE

MAKES ONE 9-INCH CAKE

3 sticks salted butter

¾ cup granulated sugar

½ teaspoon iodized salt

1 teaspoon espresso extract

2 tablespoons hot coffee

1 pound dark chocolate, finely chopped

6 eggs, at room temperature

6 egg yolks, at room temperature

Place butter, sugar, salt, espresso extract, and coffee in a small saucepan. Bring to a boil, then remove from heat. Stir in chocolate and whisk until shiny and smooth. Let rest overnight at room temperature.

The next day, bring a dozen eggs to room temperature (this takes about 1 hour). Grease a 9-inch cake pan with butter or cooking spray. Line pan with a circle of parchment paper, then grease paper as well.

Preheat oven to 350°F.

Beat eggs and yolks in a large bowl until mixed well but not foamy. Fold in chocolate mixture. Pour the batter into prepared cake pan.

Place filled cake pan inside a larger roasting pan and fill the roasting pan with hot water so that it comes about halfway up the sides. Carefully place this double pan in the oven and bake until set, about 1 hour. (The cake should be firm in the center, but still slightly wiggly.)

Remove cake from the water bath and let cool for about 30 minutes. Gently unmold and serve at room temperature.

Alternatively, this cake can be unmolded, refrigerated overnight, and served at room temperature the next day.

RED BEET VELVET CAKE

MAKES ONE 9-INCH CAKE ────────────────────────────────

2 medium beets (about 1 pound)

1¼ cups cake flour

2 tablespoons unsweetened cocoa powder (not Dutch processed)

½ teaspoon iodized salt

½ teaspoon baking powder

½ teaspoon baking soda

½ cup buttermilk

2 tablespoons lemon juice

1 tablespoon vanilla extract

1 tablespoon white wine vinegar

8 tablespoons salted butter, softened but still cool

1½ cups granulated sugar

2 eggs

1 recipe Cream Cheese Frosting (pg. 49)

Sweet Beet Chips (pg. 258), for garnish (optional)

Grated chocolate, for garnish (optional)

Preheat oven to 400°F.

Prepare the beets. Cut tops off beets and rinse well. Wrap tightly in foil. Bake until tender, about 45 minutes to 1 hour. Let cool in foil. When cool, peel skins off, cut into quarters, and purée. Set aside ½ cup beet purée for this cake.

Reduce oven temperature to 325°F. Grease two 9-inch pans with butter or cooking spray. Line each pan with a circle of parchment paper, then grease paper as well.

Make the cake. In a bowl, sift together flour, cocoa powder, salt, baking powder, and baking soda. In a separate bowl, combine beet purée, buttermilk, lemon juice, vanilla extract, and vinegar.

Using a hand mixer or stand mixer fitted with the paddle attachment, cream butter and sugar on high until very light and fluffy, about 3 to 5 minutes. Reduce speed to medium, add eggs, and mix for 2 minutes. Scrape down sides of bowl and mix for an additional minute.

Reduce speed to low. Slowly add some of the flour mixture, followed by some of the beet mixture. Continue until all the flour and beet mixtures are incorporated into a thick batter.

Spread batter equally between 2 prepared pans. Bake until skewer inserted in middle comes out dry or with moist crumbs attached, about 30 minutes. Remove from oven and cool completely.

When cool, unmold 1 cake onto a platter and smooth about 1 cup of frosting onto it. Unmold second cake and lightly press it on top of the frosting. Frost the outside of the cake and decorate with Sweet Beet Chips or grated chocolate.

SWEET BEET CHIPS

MAKES 2 CUPS

2 to 3 Chioggia beets

½ teaspoon kosher salt

¼ cup vegetable oil

1 cup granulated sugar

Preheat the oven to 275°F and line a sheet pan with parchment paper.

Wash the beets well, scrubbing with a vegetable brush if necessary.

Remove and discard the tops and peel the beets. Using a sharp knife or mandoline, cut the beets into ¹⁄₁₆-inch slices; they should be paper thin.

Place the beet slices in a large bowl and toss with the salt and oil, ensuring that all the slices are separated and coated with oil. Let slices sit for 10 minutes. (Resting helps slices keep their shape and color when baking.)

Strain off any excess oil and beet juice and arrange the slices in a single layer on the prepared sheet pan.

Bake for 35 minutes, then remove the pan from the oven and sprinkle the beets with ½ cup sugar. Turn each slice over and sprinkle with remaining sugar. Bake for another 10 to 15 minutes until beets are dried and crispy. Do not let them brown.

Use as a cake garnish or sneak them as a snack. These chips will keep in an airtight container for 3 days.

EGGNOG CINNAMON CHIP SCONES

MAKES 8 SCONES

2⅓ cups all-purpose flour

3 tablespoons granulated sugar

1 tablespoon baking powder

1 teaspoon iodized salt

1 tablespoon ground cinnamon

1 teaspoon ground nutmeg

6 tablespoons salted butter, cubed, cold

1 cup cinnamon chips

1 cup eggnog, plus more for brushing

2 teaspoons vanilla extract

2 tablespoons cinnamon sugar

Preheat oven to 350°F and line a baking sheet with parchment paper.

Combine flour, sugar, baking powder, salt, cinnamon, and nutmeg in a food processor and pulse 2 times.

Add butter and pulse until it is incorporated and the mixture resembles a coarse meal, about 10 to 15 pulses. Dump mixture into a large mixing bowl. Stir in cinnamon chips. Very quickly and gently stir in 1 cup eggnog and vanilla extract, being careful not to over mix.

Form dough into a flattened round ball. If it is too sticky to handle, sprinkle with flour. Flatten into a 1-inch-thick disk. Cut into 8 equal wedges and place on a parchment-lined baking sheet. Brush the tops of each scone with remaining eggnog, then sprinkle with cinnamon sugar.

Bake for 12 minutes, rotate the pan, and continue baking for about 10 more minutes. Scones are done when they are golden brown and spring back lightly when pressed gently in the middle.

WINTER BEET OLD FASHIONED

Tim Grejtak

Shrubs may be new to cocktail drinkers today, but they are as old as colonial New England itself. Prior to the invention of canning or refrigeration, vinegar—being cheaper and more available than sugar or citrus in the Colonies—was often used to preserve fruits and vegetables after harvest because of its strong acidity. Over time, the vinegar would become infused with flavor, strained off, mixed with some sugar and rum, and served as an early version of a cocktail.

We continue this tradition with this simple winter cocktail that is packed with complex flavor. Smoky bourbon and herbal Averna meld with our sweet-and-sour beet shrub to create a drink that lingers on the palate. The rosemary garnish adds a festive feel that is well suited for any holiday dinner, and the beautiful deep red color is perfect for Valentines' Day. This is a wonderful, warming cocktail to enjoy through the snowy months.

MAKES 1 DRINK

BEET SHRUB
MAKES 12 OUNCES

2 medium red beets (about 1 pound)

½ cup white vinegar

½ cup apple cider vinegar

¼ cup granulated sugar

COCKTAIL

2 ounces bourbon

1 ounce Averna

1 ounce Beet Shrub

1 sprig rosemary

Chill cocktail tumbler in the freezer.

Make Beet Shrub. Wash beets, remove leaves, and cut beets into medium cubes.

In food processor or blender, purée beets with vinegars and sugar for about 30 seconds. Strain into a medium bowl, pressing out remaining liquid from beets. Set strained shrub aside. Beet Shrub will keep in the refrigerator for up to 1 month.

Add bourbon, Averna, Beet Shrub, and ice to cocktail shaker and stir for 30 seconds.

Strain into a chilled cocktail tumbler.

Garnish drink with rosemary sprig.

ACKNOWLEDGMENTS

This book would not have been possible without the support and dedication of the entire farm crew and our families. In addition to creating the time and space necessary for us to work on this book, they provided the encouragement to see this project through.

There are a few whose help cannot be stressed enough, notably Peter Volante, Peter & Caterina's grandson, whose extensive oral history and commitment to chronicling his family were instrumental in piecing together the Volantes' early years in America.

Likewise, Beth Fridinger (Nardone) and Frank and Jack Driscoll provided necessary information to fill the gaps in the family history as well as ample photos of these early generations.

Ferdinand's dear friend Elio Angelucci was instrumental in faithfully translating Ferdinand's heirloom recipes from the pot to the page. He, his wife Anna, and Natalia Franco translated stacks of letters and postcards sent between Ferdinand, Anne, and Eugenio, helping to piece together the family's arrival to New England.

Gratitude is also extended to David Greenway, Molly Lyne, and Linda Mauro for their written contributions, Tim Hawkridge, Kerry Bez, Susan Stewart, and Barbara Thompson for access to their extensive photo libraries, and Jamie Turbayne for sharing historic Needham artifacts, references, and knowledge.

To all of those who have supported the farm through the years, this book is a reflection of your contribution as well. Thank you for sharing our first hundred years with us.
– Ryan Conroy, Todd and Jen Heberlein, & the Volante Family

REFERENCES

Clarke, George Kuhn, A.M, LL.B. History of Needham Massachusetts 1711-1911. Cambridge, MA: University Press, 1912.

Crumbaker, Leslie G. The Baker Estate or Ridge Hill Farms of Needham. Quincy, MA: Norfolk County Development and Tourist Council, 1975.

Reagan, Gary. *The Joy of Mixology*. New York: Clarkson Potter, 2003. 213.

Smith, Everett M. "Pascal Celery—A 30-Year Secret." Christian Science Monitor (Boston), September 2, 1953.

"Vacation Farming in Florida." Christian Science Monitor (Boston), February 23, 1946.

INDEX